Advance Praise

Betsy Gall pulls no punches in this riveting, frank, and heartbreaking book. Her 49-year-old husband Matthew, a dedicated oncologist, soulmate, father, and lover of life, killed himself on Thanksgiving Day 2019. He died of untreated depression, ironically and tragically, not uncommon in ailing physicians. Ms. Gall's book is one family's journey through unspeakable loss and anguish, buttressed with courage, love, unwavering faith, determination, and hope. "The Illusion of the Perfect Profession" is also a clarion call to the world of medicine that all physicians with psychiatric illnesses have a right to life-saving care without having to worry about their privacy and dignity or losing their job, or assaults to their medical license. Her book honors her husband. It is a gift and warrants a wide readership.

~Michael F Myers, MD Professor of Clinical Psychiatry, SUNY Downstate Health Sciences University, Brooklyn, New York, and author of "Why Physicians Die by Suicide: Lessons Learned from Their Families and Others Who Cared."

Betsy Gall's heartfelt book about the suicide of her physician husband and its aftermath offers thoughtful insights, first-hand observations, and personal advice, all written with love and understanding. Her book will be of immense help to survivors of suicide loss as well as the medical community.

~Carla Fine, author of *No Time to Say Goodbye: Surviving the Suicide of a Loved One*

The Illusion of the Perfect Profession

Bill ~

Thanks so much
for the love & support!

Blessings ~

Betsy

THE ILLUSION

of the

PERFECT PROFESSION

One wife's story about love, physician
suicide, and finding comfort and purpose
in the aftermath

BETSY GALL

First Printing: November 2022
First Edition

Paperback: 978-1-952976-93-3
eBook: 978-1-952976-94-0
Hardcover: 978-1-952976-95-7
LCCN: 2022920862

Cover and interior design by Ann Aubitz
Headshot by Dietrich Gesk
Photos are from the Gall family photo collection unless otherwise noted.

Published by Kirk House Publishers
1250 E 115th Street
Burnsville, MN 55337
Kirkhousepublishers.com
612-781-2815

Dedication

This book is dedicated to all of the doctors in the world that go into the profession of medicine to help and to heal the sick. Please take care of yourselves—the world needs you.

This book is also dedicated to my three amazing children Grady, Gavin, and Sophie. Don't ever stop being the sweet, sensitive, caring souls that you are. You are all not only brave but kind. Continue to let your light shine!

And, of course, this book is dedicated to my late husband, Dr. Matthew Taylor Gall, who put being a doctor first above all else. We will forever miss Dad, fun guy, the Gallster...you saved lives while here on earth, and I know you're continuing to do so in heaven.

Table of Contents

Introduction

I t's 3 a.m. on Thanksgiving morning—the bedroom is dark. I'm scared, and my heart is beating out of my chest. I woke up to Matthew saying, "What's going to happen, Bets?"

Oh, dear Lord, I thought to myself, *the sleep medication didn't work. Why Lord, why didn't it work?* My husband Matthew was very sick. He was suicidal last night.

Last night, Chris, my brother-in-law, was trying desperately to pry open our master bathroom door in order to get Matt to hand over the small, silver handgun he was holding. Matt was wearing a beautiful blue dress shirt. My husband always prided himself on dressing impeccably, and today was no exception. We had planned on remodeling this house, but things here in North Carolina have "gone south" quickly, so I'd simply had the bathroom painted white, making it feel clean and bright.

Matthew kept asking, "Is Sophie home?" And he repeatedly said, "It's over. It's over." Sophie is our 13-year-old daughter, and her bedroom is directly above our master bathroom. "Yes, she is home," I said. Diane, my sweet, red-headed sister-in-law was pacing outside the bedroom door. "I'm going to call 911," she kept repeating. I said, "Matthew, you are a child of God. You are a child of God!" The look on Chris's face was panicked and pained. Sweat beads were rolling down his forehead. He didn't have half the strength of my husband.

Matthew is my muscular, powerful, brilliant partner of 20 years. He has the strongest mind and the strongest body. *How did we get here?* I thought to myself. Grady suddenly walked down the hallway. "Grady! Grady, Dad has a gun. Can you help?" I pleaded. Grady, my beautiful, handsome 17-year-old boy, walked up to the door and said, "Dad...Dad... I've been there. I understand how you feel. Please don't do this. Open the door."

"Enough!" I screamed. "THIS IS OVER!" Chris looked at me, with a petrified look on his face. "Matthew, this is OVER!" I yelled. Grady and Chris pushed open the door and got the gun out of Matthew's hand.

I'm floating. I've been floating for about the past three months. I feel like I am in a bad made-for-TV movie. God is here though; God is with me. *What in the hell has happened to my husband? We've only been in North Carolina for three months. What has happened to our perfectly normal, beautiful, all-American life?* "Matthew, you're going to the emergency room. Chris, Di, and Grady are taking you to the ER."

I'm way too tired; I can't go. I am exhausted. Matthew hasn't slept for more than three or four hours a night for the past twelve weeks; therefore, my sleep has been irregular and cut short as well. Tomorrow is Thanksgiving, and I will have a lot to do.

I've been fighting for Matthew since mid-August. The oncology practice that Matthew recently joined is not what we thought it was going to be—and this has contributed greatly to Matthew's stress. Everything that could go wrong has. I have a plan to get us out of this situation, but Matthew has to stay with me. *I can't lose him*, I think to myself.

Off they go to the emergency room, about ten minutes away from our home. They drive off in Chris and Di's big, baby-blue Cadillac. They are taking my husband, a physician, who has never suffered from depression or even believed in depression for that matter, to the ER because he is suicidal. Matt had once told our oldest son Grady, "Don't use your depression as a crutch." And he also told him that "Suicide is for cowards."

This is not a joke. Matthew Taylor Gall, age 49, MD, MS, was threatening to kill himself. I have to ask myself, *"How, God? How did this become my life?"*

Chapter 1
Becoming a Doctor

This is the true story of my life. I have kept journals on and off over the years. This book is based on those journals, my letters to God, and my memories. This is my journey. The words are from the heart (Godly inspired), many in the moment, and I share this tragedy with the hope that others will find help or be equipped to help and comfort others in crisis. While this is a tragic and sad true story—this is also a story of God's presence, comfort, and making a way for my children and how God made and continues makes a way for all of us. This is truly my life. We will not allow the way Matthew died to define our lives, we have hope, we have God, and we will live. Let me back up and share with you the last few decades of my life. – Betsy Gall.

While living in Chicago back in August of 1996, I started to keep a journal for myself in hopes of better understanding who I was and what I wanted out of my life.

I wrote this: *At 26 years old, I have come far, and learned a lot, but still know that I have a long journey ahead. I seek love, truth, and wisdom. Hopefully one day, I will come full circle and find these things that my heart desires.*

My girlfriends are my backbone, and they give me strength. I am lucky to have so many of them. My love life is nonexistent. I have yet to meet my prince charming. I still have faith that he is out there somewhere. Physically I am in shape, but I'd like to lose some more weight. This is a battle I am convinced will never go away. I need to find the willpower to lose these extra pounds, then maybe I'll feel better about myself.

On this Friday night, I sit alone in my room. I just watched the movie A Time to Kill. *I will not settle for anyone who is not like the character, Jake. I think he is a ten-plus guy. Where are the men like him? I think I deserve to love someone of that caliber. And he, too, should be lucky to love me. I have faith that one day it will happen. Please God, let it happen.*

All of my friends are in love, and I'm happy for every one of them. They deserve the best. Sarah, my best friend from college, really understands me. We are in the same boat. Volunteering puts everything into perspective. Helping these children that live in the run-down inner-city housing projects reminds me of this. I'm grateful to live the life I do. I need to remember that I can only find happiness from within. I want to fall in love. I have to keep the faith and lead a healthy life. Eating well and exercising is important to me. I love my family and my friends.

September 1996, and it's Labor Day Weekend. I should have gone back to Minneapolis. I want to be with my family. I want to laugh and tell stories. I miss them. I am here only because I am participating in a triathlon. I want to find someone to confide in and laugh with and be best friends with. I don't have a partner to do that with. I want to meet the right guy. God, make it happen, soon please!

Everyone I know is married or getting married. My life sucks—but I know that one day the perfect guy will come. Then I doubt again, and even though I want to fall in love and get married and have kids, I sometimes think, Maybe it's not in the cards for me?

My girlfriends were in town last weekend, we had fun at a local watering hole. It was there that I met this doctor named Matthew. He seems cool. He has a great voice, and he called me on Saturday night. A few days later, I had a date with the cute doctor. He is really unique; he's funny and I can tell he has a big heart. He has lots of friends. He seems like a good guy. He's passionate about lots of things, like music, food, and football, he is an over-the-top Steeler fan, but he is mostly passionate about being a doctor.

March of 1997, and I have been dating Matt for a little over four months. He is extremely dedicated and spends so much of his time at the hospital. We spent four days together in Michigan, where we skied and had a wonderful time. I did notice that he dipped a piece of cheese into cheese dip. I'm guessing this must be a Wisconsin thing.

Matthew is at the hospital a lot, but when he's not, we really enjoy being together. We are both falling in love, and last weekend we told each other, "I love you." Things have seemed to fall into place. He's from such a fantastic family. I love spending quality time with him. I want a husband, a dog, a house, and a baby. I believe that everything is better in your life when you are in love!

It's August 1997, and Matthew has been studying like crazy because he has a big medical exam coming up. He told me that we are important, and we will make it through this. Matt and I like the same things. We want happy, healthy lives, success, and the picture-perfect marriage. Matthew is the best. I can't imagine my life without him.

Love is all that matters. I am blessed to have the love from my family, friends, and Matthew. I am dedicated to making my life the best ever.

It's a dark, cold Chicago November evening. Matt is home from the hospital, and he's exhausted. I love being with him every single second. He is very sweet, loving, honest, caring, and sexy. Having Matthew in my life makes everything else seem okay. I know my time will come—but patience has never been my strong suit.

Matt had asked me to go to dinner with him on Saturday night in July of 1998...but I had other plans. "Beth is coming to town," I said. Beth is one of my best friends from high school.

We are having a "girls' day," then will probably go out on the town. "Maybe we'll catch up later," I told him.

My girls' day started at 10 a.m. when I picked Beth up from her sister's apartment and we went for a long walk on the beach. As usual, we got caught up and talked about our lives, men, and marriage. From there we went for a casual lunch. Beth looked at me and said, "I have something for you." She proceeded to hand me a letter addressed Betsy #1.

"What is this?" I asked. I opened the envelope she handed me to find a letter from my boyfriend, Matthew. When I realized that Matthew was sending me on a scavenger hunt all over the city, I started crying, because basically I knew that Matthew was going to propose. I apparently had to go to the salon for hair and makeup, then to Michigan Avenue to buy a new dress. Beth and I hugged and screamed a little as I jumped for joy. I thanked Beth for being such a good friend, and off I went. Little did I know that behind the scenes, Matthew was praying that none of his credit cards would be declined while I was on this pricy scavenger hunt.

Cleaned up, with a new cute black dress and heels on, I headed to the 95th floor of the John Hancock building. I was told to go to the bar upstairs. I looked furiously for Matthew, but I couldn't find him. I felt a bit disappointed. I thought maybe he chickened out—he wasn't there. And then he stood up and waved. I moved toward him—and it felt as if we were the only two people that existed. He gave me a hug and told me that I looked beautiful. We were seated at a table overlooking Lake

Michigan and a beautiful downtown skyline. A rainbow appeared. Truly, it could have not been more perfect. We ate dinner; he had a steak and I had lobster. We drank good wine and talked about our relationship—we reminisced about the first night we met, all of the dates, the laughter, and the love.

When we left the Hancock around 8 p.m., I asked Matthew if we could go meet Beth and the girls. He said sure, that his car was parked across the street. As we walked hand in hand, we passed the Four Seasons Hotel. He asked if I'd ever stayed there, and I sarcastically replied, "Oh yes, right, all of the time." He persuaded me to go inside and check it out. We went up to the 45th floor, where he'd reserved the executive suite. He told me to wait outside the door. Now I was nervous and had butterflies in my stomach. A couple of minutes later, he called my name. I open the first door to find a pathway of rose petals in a candle-lit room. Soft music was playing in the background. I walked up to a set of closed French doors. I opened them to find Matthew on one knee holding the most gorgeous princess cut diamond ring. He said, "Betsy, I love you more than anything...will you be my wife?" I started crying, laughing, and screaming. I gave him a hug and a huge kiss and said "YES, with all of my heart." We cracked the Dom Perignon that he had chilling.

I called my parents, who'd been expecting the call. They were actually watching Father of the Bride" the Steve Martin movie. Then we called Matthew's parents. Matt told me that there was one more thing. So we left the fancy suite and went downstairs to a waiting white stretch limousine. We drove all *over the city. We drove to our favorite spots as we kissed and laughed. It happened to be Venetian night in Chicago, and fireworks were going off. It was spectacular. We then proceed to pick up my girlfriends and party in the limo. We got dropped off at the Four Seasons around 1 a.m.*

Well, that was my night—our greatest night so far. I know with a romantic like Matthew, things will forever be amazing!

The Early Years

Matthew did not come from a family of doctors. He was a bright child from a small town in Wisconsin. His parents recall that he was a *very* energetic kid. In fact, his mom, Elaine, would joke that if she'd had Matthew first, there wouldn't have been a second child. She had Chris first, five years Matt's senior. Matthew was a precocious and thrill-seeking child. He was always climbing on top of the refrigerator or biking very fast down the street. He learned to read at a young age. People apparently always told him that he was extremely smart and that he should become a doctor—so that's what he decided to do.

Matthew was a popular guy while in high school. He volunteered at Lutheran Hospital, meeting with elderly residents in the hospital where he was born. He was student council president, he was a Christian, and he had integrity. Matt always stood up for the underdog. Matthew earned various academic recognition awards. He was junior prom king, captain of his high school football team, and he played rugby as a "Badger" at UW Madison. Matthew did joke about having nine concussions over the course of his lifetime. Looking back, this is nothing to joke about.

Matthew was a 1992 graduate of the University of Wisconsin Madison with degrees in biochemistry and molecular biology. He was a Badger through and through. Matt would run up and down the stands of Camp Randall Stadium dressed as the Ultimate Badger Warrior, waving a UW flag while wearing face paint, a red speedo, and donning a wig. This guy was self-assured; whereas I was embarrassed by these images, he was proud. He had so much self-confidence, and it was always on display.

Matt was a 1996 graduate of the Medical College of Wisconsin with a doctorate in medicine. He did his internship and residency at The University of Illinois Chicago. He was a 2003 graduate of the University of Minnesota Twin Cities, with a fellowship in oncology and hematology and a master's degree in clinical research.

When I first met Matthew at that bar in Lincoln Park, a young, trendy part of Chicago, he was overly confident and hilarious. Matt was doing his surgical rotation at UIC in Chicago. He would work sixteen hours a day and be off for eight hours. It was brutal and he was mostly exhausted, his skin had a light green tinge to it, and he had dark circles under his eyes. But man, did that guy have stamina. Matthew was a force to be reckoned with because he believed that he could do anything he put his mind to.

And he did put his mind to medicine. When we met, he was doing a surgical rotation, but he decided not to become a surgeon after all. He chose hematology and oncology, and I knew that would be a great fit for Matthew because he was such a sensitive and caring soul. He was very compassionate, had such a big heart—and saw hope and optimism in the field of oncology.

Matthew loved his cancer patients, and most of them loved him. He'd come home with gifts from these special patients—like flowers, hand-knit baby blankets, wine, chocolate, and lots of Salted Nut Rolls, his favorite candy bar. He was close with his patients, but I guess you have to be when dealing with such an invasive, life-altering disease like cancer. Matthew was even known to pray with his fellow Christian patients. He'd come home after a long day and explain these special encounters to me.

Matthew and I got married in my hometown of Edina, Minnesota, on September 4, 1999. It was a beautiful wedding. It was hot and sticky that day, especially for Minnesota. St. Stephen's Episcopal Church looks like it could be in Europe. It has a pretty grey stone façade and sits looking over a rambling creek on the corner of Wooddale and 50th street. I was baptized in that church, and I used to attend Girl Scouts in the basement when I was in the third grade. I grew up around the corner in the historic neighborhood dubbed "country club," thus St. Stephen's had always held a special place in my heart.

Friends came from all over the country to attend our wedding. It was a picture-perfect day that I'll never forget. The chubby minister, with his rosy cheeks, took both of our hands, and with his British accent, stated, "What God has joined together, let no man put asunder." And then we turned to look out at all of our family and friends, and while he pronounced us husband and wife, we had a fabulous kiss. Then he presented us, "I happily present to you Dr. and Mrs. Matthew Gall."

It was a fantastic day. As we climbed into the white Mercedes Benz convertible and headed over to our reception at Interlachen Country Club, I'll never forget thinking to myself: *I want to have the perfect life with this man.* I sat in that car in my strapless white wedding dress, veil flowing in the open air, and I thought, *I know we will be happy, and we will have the best life.* A photo of us leaving the church even appeared in *Minnesota Bride* magazine. How perfect is that?

And it truly was mostly a happy life in the beginning. After our wedding, Matthew and I went back to Chicago, where he would finish up his residency training. Since his decision to become an oncologist, he had applied to several fellowship programs across the country. After it was all said and done, he decided to train at the University of

Minnesota. Now, after I had spent seven years in Chicago, we decided to move back to my hometown, Minneapolis.

In retrospect...

I thought being married to a doctor would be life on easy street. I was wrong. Becoming a doctor isn't easy. Medical schools are highly competitive. The national acceptance rate is 43 percent, according to data compiled by the Association of American Medical Colleges. Matthew had fun in college, but he was highly driven. He didn't join a fraternity because he knew he wouldn't be able to handle the party aspect. He always kept his eye on the prize—and the prize for Matthew was getting into med school.

I didn't know Matthew back when he had applied to only one medical school—where he was promptly waitlisted. He talked about being devastated about that. His family was in tears when they heard the news. Matt had worked hard his entire life—and then he was waitlisted. Reflecting upon Matthew's early life, I understand that he didn't face much adversity, other than this setback.

So in 1992, Matt took a job at a lab and had been living in Chicago for about a week when he happened to call his old roommate back in Madison, Wisconsin. Thank God he did. The roommate very casually said, "Oh Gallster, there is a message on the machine from the Medical College of Wisconsin. You've got to call them back by the end of the day today if you want a med school spot. They are holding one for you." Omigosh…really? This guy didn't even think about calling Matt to relay the message? It didn't matter. Matthew's prayer had been answered. His hard work was finally going to pay off—he was in! He packed up the next day and moved to Milwaukee, leaving Chicago in the rearview mirror.

Medical school is expensive. The median cost of four years of medical school attendance in 2019–2020 was $250,222 at public institutions and $330,180 at private colleges, according to a fall 2020 report issued by the Association of American Medical Colleges.

That's just med school! First of all, you have to get accepted, and second of all, you need to find a way to pay for it—all this on top of one's undergraduate studies.

I didn't know Matthew in medical school. I do know that he spent long hours at the library. He told some funny stories, mostly about how broke he was. He'd eat or "share" as he'd say (a.k.a. steal) his roommate's food. He wasn't happy with the neighbor's dog that constantly barked, interrupting his studies. He was always wearing noise-canceling headphones around the house.

Specializing in hematology/oncology requires a fellowship, which is an accredited training program that requires three years of additional training once the basic three (or four) years of internal medicine residency is completed. People are surprised to find out that it takes an extremely long time to become a doctor. It's an absolute minimum of ten years following high school, but it is not unusual for it to take twelve to fourteen years, depending on one's chosen specialty. It was a total of fourteen years *after high school* for Matthew to complete his training.

Chapter 2
A Doctor's Life

I am going to try to briefly explain a doctor's life—but if you have a doctor in the family—or are already dating or married to one, you know what it is like. Hopefully others will understand how excruciating and demanding this work is, and how it can be extremely stressful.

People training to be a medical doctor are given different titles as they progress through the medical ranks. They begin as medical students, then progress to interns, residents, and eventually fellows. Once residency and fellowship trainings are complete, a person can become a board-certified attending physician.

The "attending" physician is the medical doctor who has completed all training. They are board-certified and are responsible for the overall care of patients in a hospital or clinic setting. An attending physician may also teach and supervise residents, medical students, and interns involved in patient care.

"On call" can mean different things, depending on what type of physician you are. For resident doctors, on call typically means staying in the hospital overnight to care for patients as needed. It can also mean taking calls from home. There isn't a typical on-call shift.

Because of its complexity, on-call work may involve working beyond regular hours or shifts, meaning typically nights and holidays. I'm dating myself here, but in the beginning, Matthew had a pager—and took page requests (calls) from other hospital staff to help with patient care, assisting other doctors and nurses with their duties and responsibilities. He had to be in close proximity to the hospital and not have any other activities scheduled for that time. Matt was not a fan of that pager. He detested it.

Obviously, on-call work can look very different, depending on one's field. Certain specialties may not require a ton of on-call work, especially those that have limited emergencies, like dermatology. Other specialties, like surgery or anesthesia, may be particularly exasperating. Most on-call doctors are overwhelmed by the workload and can become easily fatigued, especially on long overnight shifts.

The biggest challenges can include stamina—or just being able to stay alert working such long hours—and competence, being able to maintain quality care in the face of possible fatigue. One must also have expertise; they must have wide enough knowledge and experience to deal with any potential case.

One misconception surrounding on-call shifts is the idea of "home call." This requires that physicians be on hand to respond to emergency calls. The only difference is that home calls don't require the doctor to be present at the hospital or clinic. This is mainly what Matthew encountered. He would take calls from home, manage patients' care from afar, and only on a rare occasion would he have to physically go to the hospital, although it did happen from time to time.

Active residents working on call for long hours can be adversely affected by lack of sleep. Choosing a medical specialty that provides a good quality of life is a common concern for med students. How often a doctor works on call is largely dependent on what their specialty is and what the details of their contract are. Being on call for Matthew typically meant doing patient rounds in the hospital during the morning weekend hours, as well as taking calls from home.

Beyond that, there's no one answer. On-call hours are determined by a hospital-doctor basis, and they differ across all institutions. Rural doctors, and those in understaffed areas, could possibly expect more on-call work. How often a doctor gets called tends to depend on medical specialty. One common confusion about being on call is that doctors and other healthcare workers get paid more for working it. This isn't always the case.

According to some data I read, around 60 percent of hospitals offer doctors on-call pay—and how much of an increase that is, is open to debate. It's usually agreed that any stipends depend on specialty, as well as the simple economics of supply and demand.

While all of our friends were buying their first homes, Matthew and I purchased a small two-bedroom condominium in downtown Minneapolis. I was working for a cool, hip design firm in the city, and Matthew would be close to the university, where he was completing his oncology/hematology fellowship program. We loved walking to dinner and biking along the Stone Arch Bridge. I'm not going to lie; we were also jealous of our friends buying their first homes. Everyone around us seemed to be making money—and we were still just making ends meet. Matthew and I did not come from money. I grew up in an affluent neighborhood where everyone around us seemed to have more. Matthew and I both concluded that while we had idyllic childhoods, and everything we needed growing up, we wanted to provide more for our family.

We both worked really hard. Matthew decided to moonlight for extra money. In its most basic terms, moonlighting is a secondary job worked in addition to one's main, primary job. For medical residents, moonlighting may mean working as an independent physician, outside of the scope of your residency training program. There's also a difference between internal moonlighting—working in the same facility as your primary position—and external moonlighting, or working outside of it.

So even though he worked his tail off during the week, Matthew picked up shift work at the Veterans Administration or another local hospital on evenings and weekends.

Matthew was such a dedicated, hard worker. I tell anyone who thinks that doctors make too much money that they're nuts. I've seen first-hand the sacrifice these young men and women make in order to be able to help people throughout their careers. If anything, they should make *more* money as a thank you. Some healthcare CEOs can make upward of $10-plus million dollars a year, while some of our physicians who sacrifice *everything* are struggling to make ends meet. I am disgusted as to what we value in society today.

Matthew was 32 years old when he started to make "real" money, and we still had to pay off our ginormous medical school debt. Even though his parents helped with essential needs during those med school days, our debt was significant. I say "ours" because when you get married and team up like Matt and I did—the debt became mine, too. I worked hard to get our finances in order. Matthew previously had no choice but to "steal from Peter to pay Paul." His finances were a mess when we first got together; he'd take money out on his credit card to pay the rent. I was the breadwinner during this time and was working full-time as a senior project manager for a firm that designed all of the top restaurants in Minneapolis. It was exciting and rewarding work, and I enjoyed it immensely, but I knew eventually that I wanted to have children and stay home to raise my family.

Luckily having a baby didn't take too long for us. Our son Grady was born on April 5, 2002. Matthew was, of course, moonlighting the night my water broke. I had to have my parents pick me up and take me to Hennepin County Medical Center while Matthew finished his shift. I'll never forget Matthew was so nervous and sleep-deprived that when we left the hospital with our newborn son, he started driving the wrong way down a one-way street.

Grady was the apple of his father's eye. We adored our son. Grady was, and still is, a beautiful, kind human being who is easy to love.

After the fellowship program was complete, Matthew was hired by the leading, prominent private practice in town, and they were wonderful to us. Matthew absolutely loved his mentor and senior partner, and he and his wife became true, steadfast friends. When Matthew was hired, they threw a beautiful party to introduce us to the other partners within what I'll call for this book...The Group.

This kind doctor was always the voice of reason with his calm disposition, and Matthew truly admired him.

A simple life with a good routine was quickly settling in as Matthew set up his practice in a suburb of Minneapolis, Minnesota. Eventually, a junior partner came along, and the team of three worked well together in their thriving private practice. Busy long days were normal, but Matthew really loved his patients, and loved working in that clinic.

By now, space at the condo was becoming tight. Somehow Matthew and I were able to pull off building our dream house out in the suburbs in 2003. This was actually all Matthew's doing. I didn't think we could afford it, but once again he put forth his determination, and nothing could stop him. It didn't hurt that this was 2002, and the banks were very generous with home loans and mortgages, especially to promising young doctors.

Building the house made Matthew happy. We finally had space, and a yard, and I felt lucky and privileged to finally be able to design a home specifically for our family. My vision of the perfect life was certainly falling into place.

Matthew loved being in private practice. He liked having at least a little control and say in how things were run. Doctors nowadays have to report to hospital administrators—"suits" as Matthew referred to them—and let's be honest, the "suits" didn't go to medical school. Doctors are on the front lines, and they know best what patients need.

Matthew wanted to be involved and take on leadership roles within his practice, and even though he worked really long hours, and took call every other week or so, Matthew served many roles over his tenure with The Group. He was chief of staff at the local hospital, he served on the Political Action Committee, the Cancer Committee, the Finance Committee, and the Board of Directors for The Group. He was super busy, and was managing a lot.

I truly didn't understand the pressure that our doctors are under until I was married to one. There was just so much pressure. Medicine is also a big business, on top of caring for the sick. The threat of a hospital takeover was real, and Matthew didn't like that possibility one bit.

On November 13, 2004, I was in labor a second time. Again, Matthew was on call but at home, and had just fallen asleep. I didn't want to wake Matthew until I absolutely had to. Sleep was important to him, and let's say he could be a little crabby while on call. To this day, I've yet to meet a doctor who likes taking call. That being said, he wasn't exactly thrilled when I woke him up. Thankfully for us, the senior partner was there to cover the rest of Matthew's call shift. Matthew was actually able to drive me to the hospital that night, where I delivered our beautiful bouncing 10-pound baby boy the next day. Gavin had an easy disposition, and he was and still is a joy. I loved the fact that I was Mom to two healthy boys.

Happy, full, busy, extremely active, and fun days consumed us while living at our dream home. Matthew and I had befriended several neighbors. We hosted numerous neighborhood gatherings. I was able to quit my job officially—but because I loved to work, I consulted on the side, from time to time. Matthew and I considered ourselves financially conservative, so we were ecstatic when we were *finally* able to pay off our huge medical school debt. Now I was able to decorate the house, and we took some fabulous family vacations once he made partner at The Group. It seemed as though life was playing out as I had envisioned it would. Finally!

Then, on April 7, 2006, Sophia Elizabeth made us parents again. This time Matthew had just finished being on call and was able to meet me at my scheduled induction at Southdale Fairview Hospital. He wore a blue dress shirt because we thought for sure another boy was on his way. When my OB/GYN pulled out our daughter, Matthew looked at her and stuttered, "Is it, is it...really a girl?" Her reply, "Are you really a doctor, Matthew?" We had a good laugh at this one.

So our family was complete. Sophie had (and still has) a big, loving personality. She was and continues to be our darling sunshine. I'd always dreamed of having two boys and a girl. God delivered—and we were grateful—with three healthy kids, a gorgeous house, parents and siblings all living within five hours of each other. Life was good. On top of it, Matthew and I had tons of friends. We threw some lively parties; we both absolutely loved to entertain. Our house was the hub of entertainment.

In 2009, Matthew and I had saved enough money to purchase a small lake house in northern Minnesota. We both love the outdoors and enjoyed mountain biking, boating, waterskiing, and relaxing by the lake. Our little place at the end of a peninsula was nothing fancy but had everything on our wish list. It had a long, wooded private drive in, over 270 feet of west-facing lakeshore, and it was cute but not too cute so that we'd feel bad tearing it down one day to build our retirement home. Matthew loved the lake house immensely and referred to it as "My happy place." Matthew found joy and peace at the lake that he couldn't find living in the suburbs.

We had to complete our perfect life now with one more addition. An adorable British crème golden retriever named Liberty joined our family in 2013. My gosh, I cannot even begin to explain how this puppy added pure joy to our lives.

There we were—we were living a wonderful, fun-filled, all-American life. I was a stay-at-home mom, with three healthy children, and was married to an oncologist. We finally had money in the bank, a second place on a lake to call home, and I was thankful and content.

The pressures of work were constant for Matthew. He didn't always have the best time-management skills, so when he was rushed, watch out. He prided himself on efficiency. He also was a perfectionist. I didn't realize it fully until we had *two* lawns to take care of. Matthew loved taking care of the lawn. This was time for him to be outside, get a workout, and see the fruits of his labor. He wore headphones and knee pads and jammed out to his favorite 80's rock bands. He spent countless hours on the lawn. I would barely park the car at our lake house before he'd jump out of the car to start blowing the leaves. Let's just say he was obsessed with the lawn.

I learned early on that everyone knows someone with cancer. Everyone has a brother, a mother, a sister, or a friend that has been diagnosed with cancer—and these friends would call asking Matthew about treatment plans, a diagnosis, or what to do next—and, could he explain things to them in layman's terms? The list goes on and on. Even though Matt may not have been officially on call for The Group every single night, he was always on call for friends, and seemed honored to be able to help. He'd lend an ear, give advice, or be that shoulder to cry on. Matthew was always there for his friends.

The early years at The Group proved to be quite lucrative. Matthew's group was largely making money, and this afforded us the luxury of not only owning two homes, but it also gave us the ability to send our kids to private school. I'd never really thought about this before we had kids, as both Matthew and I grew up in average middle-class families. We both attended public schools—and I thought we turned out okay. I remember sitting at a party at a doctor friend's home, and all of the doctors were talking about their children's educations. Everyone seemed to send their kids to private school. It felt as though it was a bit of a prerequisite—and was expected of us. Looking back, I wish we'd never gone that route.

It wasn't easy for my kids at their private school, not only because the curriculum was extremely rigorous, and we weren't Catholic, but the rules were strict. I believed there was too much pressure for them to be the best and maintain good grades. We did like the Christian aspect; I often said I would take all the help I could get in that department. But while Matthew and I both had fathers that were Catholic (Matt's practicing, mine was not), we did not raise our kids Catholic. But the children looked cute in their perfectly adorable uniforms. This added to my skewed vision of what perfect was at the time. The pressure to keep up with the Joneses is real, and it's intense.

We had no idea that our son Grady was getting severely bullied at this school—and we were blindsided and very disturbed when we found out. "It's too much," I pleaded with Matthew. "It's not only too expensive and too much pressure on these kids, but I feel as though it's ruining Grady." I wanted to pull them—but Matthew did not, asking, "What will people think?" I really didn't care what people thought, but Matt had an image to uphold. He'd been proud that he'd been able to send his kids to what we thought at the time was "the best school."

I eventually won. We pulled all three kids out at the end of the year. It was hard. Grady was happy to leave, but the other two didn't understand. It was very difficult for me, too. I'd spent years volunteering, running their gala, and pitching the school to new potential families. It was hard letting go, but we did it.

Chapter 3

What Aspects Did Matthew Struggle With?

What I think was the most significant struggle for Matthew being an oncologist was watching his patients die. I think every single death took a little piece of his heart. I'll never forget when one of my parents' best friends, John, wasn't feeling well, and he went to see Matthew. Matthew diagnosed John with cancer and John eventually died. On the way to his funeral, Matthew looked at me and said, "Do you think John's wife is mad at me?"

I was shocked at this question and stated, "Absolutely not! Matthew, he had *cancer*." I think Matthew felt that it was his duty to save everyone. He did feel like he was doing God's work. Egotism is a common trait among doctors. I really think he thought that he should be able to save every patient. Realistically, this just isn't possible, but it ate away at him. Like most physicians, he was much more sensitive than he let on to be.

Around 2013, things with The Group had shifted. Matt wasn't a fan of The Group's new president—and this guy wasn't a fan of Matthew either. Political turmoil was evident, and the potential looming changes frightened Matt.

There was also competition threatening the practice, specifically at his clinic site. As mentioned, medicine is a serious business, and The Group was consistently a target for hospital takeover. Matt didn't like this one bit.

Reimbursements were down, Matthew's salary started declining—and this really stressed him out. His group was partially production-based, and Matt had always been a top producer. Matthew worked hard to build his practice. He prided himself on efficiency and getting stuff done. He put pressure on himself to see more patients in a shorter amount of time. When Matt was rushed, he could become short with people. I'd say the majority of Matthew's patients absolutely loved him, but the saying "you can't please all of the people all of the time" rang true in his case. Matthew's bedside manner may not have *always* been the best, but I knew that his heart was in the right place—Matt's sometimes gruff manner didn't go over well with some patients and staff—and Matt heard about it from HR. In 2015, The Group sent Matthew warning letters and set him up with an executive life coach to try and help Matthew better balance his work life. Matthew had to go in front of a review committee, and he was embarrassed about this, as he didn't like to show weakness or imperfection of any form. After all, that is how they are trained in medical school.

In 2015, I obtained my real estate license, which had always been a dream of mine. Because Matthew's salary had been declining, I felt I had to do more to contribute. I'd dreamed of flipping houses as a little girl, before flipping houses was even a thing. I'd walk around my childhood neighborhood and look at houses and think to myself, *That house is cute, but it'd be* really *cute if they just added flower boxes or changed the paint color.* Matt and I used to joke and compare notes when one of us had a bad day at the office. Picking paint colors and looking at pretty houses always paled in comparison to dealing with cancer, death, and sometimes dying.

Because of the flexibility of my job, I was lucky enough to be able to attend the life coach counseling sessions, which I loved. I like learning about how and why we act a certain way. I'm constantly looking for ways to improve myself. It was tougher for Matthew because he didn't really recognize his flaws. Matthew prided himself on being a physician—and he liked thinking he was the smartest guy in the room. But we all have flaws, and we are all human. Matthew's biggest flaw was that he wasn't self-aware. He didn't see himself or hear himself the way others sometimes did. Matthew knew what was best for his patients, but the way he delivered that message of care, well, at times it could be taken the wrong way. He could be rude to staff, a little arrogant for sure, but I truly think he didn't mean any harm—because he thought his way was the best way for them. The life coach was helping Matthew try to understand this.

Matt complained about having to go see the life coach on our way to every single appointment, but I could see the difference it was making with his disposition, and it was slowly helping. It took time, years to be honest, but I was so grateful to be able to attend these sessions with Matthew. Matthew bought a book, *Handbook for Happiness*, by Dr. Amit Sood. It's a step-by-step plan for resilient living and provides instruction on how to better regulate thoughts and perceptions. I thought it was sort of sad that he had this book because being happy had always come easy for me.

Later on, I found these notes on Matthew's phone about his sessions with our life coach:

- Ask open-ended questions.
- Validate them.
- Not content, it's how you make them feel. It's often tone.
- Relationship conveys tone, 90 percent of communication is process.
- It's how you respond in the moment.
- Slow down and adjust along the way.

- Work on Achilles' heel: economy of speech, make an impact, stay in the moment.
- In order to speed up, you need to slow down.
- Thinking fast and slow.
- Be here now.
- Benevolence.
- Listen *and* hear.
- Take it in and acknowledge it.
- You being in charge of you.
- Accept that I'm not perfect.
- Emotion is contagious.

Reflecting now, this makes me sad for Matthew. These things didn't come naturally for him. And I wonder if Matt had secretly struggled with depression—but just never told me? He'd always been a pretty happy guy. He really was trying to better himself. I think spouses should be involved because we are the ones behind the scenes who know what's truly going on. I was grateful to The Group for allowing me to attend these sessions. The saying goes, "Happy wife, happy life." But I think the same could be said for husbands. That being said, I often reminded Matthew, "There are lots of other groups out there, Matt. If you don't want to stay with this group, look around for another job." Because I want to be clear, these sessions with the life coach were not optional, and it was emotionally challenging for Matthew.

Matthew did not have time to research other groups or explore other employment opportunities. We'd get postcards and calls from recruiters several times a week. I was the one who dreamed about moving to a destination with warmer weather. Minnesota winters were getting *very* old. I slipped on the ice while walking the dog. I came home frustrated, cold, and my eyelashes were literally frozen. Matthew and I loved traveling the world; we loved a good adventure, so the thought of starting over in a new warmer destination excited me.

Eventually, Matthew slowly began to put his feelers out, and he interviewed at four other private practices all over the country over the course of a few years. He received an offer from every single group he interviewed with. Nothing was "perfect," he'd say. For example, one hospital only offered small cubicles to their physicians, not a private office as Matthew was accustomed to. One position was located in a less-than-desirable location; the other just didn't feel "right."

It was in 2017 when we transferred Grady to public high school when he was a sophomore—never an easy situation for a teenager, especially for a kid who had been bullied for the past several years. At first, Grady was doing great. His grades were still good, and he joined the track team. But when he became a junior, things took a downward turn, and we felt Grady had slipped into the wrong crowd. He was running away and would never do anything that we asked of him. He was doing drugs and making really bad choices. His grades took a turn for the worse, and he quit the track team. This situation weighed heavily on both of our hearts. Matt had trouble accepting the fact that Grady didn't really care about school or sports. Matthew had been an outstanding student and a great athlete, so he couldn't wrap his brain around the fact that Grady was not like him when it came to these aspects. Grady and Matthew didn't see eye to eye on almost anything, and that year was particularly tumultuous. Because I was constantly caught in the middle, it was distressing and emotionally draining on me.

When you're running a busy household, have three kids and their activities and sports, also two busy careers, and life seems to be whizzing by, you can sometimes forget what is important. Relationships are what is important. Relationships were important to us both. Matt knew this, but having "stuff" had been really paramount to Matthew. Neither of us grew up with much "stuff." Matt grew up in a small town. I think having things to prove he was successful was critical for him. I also love beautiful things; I'm guilty of having loved our comfortable lifestyle, too.

There is a business end in the practice of medicine. Matthew was with a fantastic Group but being an oncologist who is surrounded by terminal illness and death for years is hard and it can change a person or cause one to build up defenses to cope with the pain of constant exposure to death, watching the process of death every day, and dealing with the reactions of remaining family members after a loved one loses the battle with cancer. Death and his work impacted Matt over the years and there were some issues at his job where it became mandatory for Matt to see a life coach to assist him with soft skills and the heaviness of the everyday practice of oncology. Matt unfortunately felt threatened by the mandatory coaching sessions and thought that he might lose his job. Matthew had actually been seeing the life coach for years, and even though he'd been improving, he was informed of a new patient complaint . This one blindsided Matthew. As part of the business end of the practice of medicine, a letter from The Group's lawyers stating: "FINAL WARNING" arrived in Matthew's inbox, he was not only deflated, but he felt defeated and was definitely torn up about this. I observed that he perceived that he was at a professional crisis point, he was isolating himself professionally and I think he felt trapped. His self-worth as a physician was impacted negatively. He took it really, really hard.

To make matters worse, Matthew had received a death threat from the son of a deceased patient—so he started carrying a gun to work. I hated that he did so, and we fought constantly about this. Never mind that the patient was an 84-year-old stage-four cancer patient with what appeared to be a terminal diagnosis, this person (apparently dealing with the deep sense of loss of a parent) wrote to a licensing board complaining about the care Matthew gave his father. The letter also condemned almost everyone this individual had come into contact with at the clinic, but the direct target was Matthew—and Matthew was distressed over this. I could only focus on what bad things could possibly happen from Matt (who had a conceal-and-carry permit) bringing a firearm to work. Matthew reminded me of the Minneapolis gynecological surgeon who was shot and killed at his home in 2013 by the son of a former patient. This death threat really messed with Matthew's head because of the stories he'd heard regarding doctors previously killed by patients or patients' family members. A lot of stressors were converging on Matthew and it became more difficult for him to focus on his passion in life—caring for those with cancer. It is truly a paradox what we all as patients expect from doctors. Doctors are not God—but patients and their families (and frankly all of us when praying for someone with cancer) literally are seeking miracles and are hoping and praying that a doctor is going deliver and make a miracle happen. This expectation, hope, and high standard can take a lot out of a human being, and with someone as big hearted as Matthew, the impact on him had become tangible and it was difficult for me as his spouse to process and try to help. I did everything that I could to support him, but I was not by his side at work to experience what he was experiencing. I did not feel totally helpless—but I did feel very limited in how I could try to fix what was putting additional stress upon Matthew.

Matt came home after an extremely difficult day at work and sat down in our beautiful light-filled family room. He looked at me with tears in his eyes and said, "I love my patients, but I hate my job." I looked at him and said, "Sweetie, there are many other jobs out there." And being the Type-A-fixer person that I am, I started looking for new positions for Matthew the next day.

I found a recruiter, and eventually Matthew decided to interview with a small, private practice in North Carolina. On the airplane while on our way for Matthew's interview, I turned to him and said, "You're going to get this job, like every other position you've applied for in the past." I also said, "Matt, I don't want to keep doing this. If you don't want this job, you'll have to figure out how to make things work in Minnesota." He completely agreed. But I remember thinking that a fresh start for everybody would be great.

Matt accepted the position without shadowing or even spending more than a full day with this new practice. He was promised a very large potential salary, and we thought we would eventually buy into this new practice and really be able to make a difference by helping build the practice up. We likened it to a "mini-group" back in its early days. We felt it was the right move. We were all super excited about the opportunity.

Matthew gave The Group his notice in March of 2019, the day before we left for what would come to be our last family vacation in Jamaica. He needed to give three months' notice. We put our house on the market the day we left for spring break. After we sold it, we moved to our lake house for a month, and left for North Carolina at the end of July so Matthew could start his new position on August 5. Matthew's one-year noncompete would go into effect once he left The Group.

August 7, 2019: It's been a while since I've written in my journal. Wow, so much has happened: quitting The Group, selling our beloved home, and living at our lake house for the month of July. Now we have moved to North Carolina. It has not been easy. The boys are sad. Gavin isn't happy about the football program here. He doesn't think he will be able to play much. Grady is doing okay, but I'll worry about him forever. He doesn't really have a passion—and he talks about his depression and anxiety a lot lately. I wish life were easier for him. I wish life was easier for all of us.

This house we purchased will be fabulous once I am finished remodeling it. Right now, it's overwhelming and intimidating to think about all that needs to be done. I can't believe I bought a house that literally has everything wrong with it. I know I can fix it up, and it will be gorgeous. We have promised the kids a pool as a way of softening the blow of such a big move across the country.

The neighborhood is fantastic—I absolutely love it. My heart is heavy, but I put on a brave face for others around me to see. Lord, please stay with me and protect us. Please help Matthew cope with this difficult job change. We've put all of our eggs into this one basket. Please let it all be good and true.

I pray that my family stays safe. Please God, watch over my family. Please bring joy and happiness to this next phase of life. Please God, I beg of you, watch over us and protect us.

I miss Sophie and I miss Liberty. Sophie is at camp, but I'm going back to Minnesota to get them in a few weeks. Right now, I'm here getting the boys settled in. I miss my old neighbors and my friends, my parents, my gym, my real estate business, and my book club, but most of all, I miss my happy kids and my happy husband. I pray: Bring them back, God, please. Please help us to find happiness and joy.

When we arrived in North Carolina back in August of 2019, it was like God wrapped his arms around me and whispered in my ear, "Buckle up Betsy, it's going to be a bumpy ride." I remember thinking to myself that I must write. I must journal every day, but more importantly, I must pray harder than I'd ever prayed. I walked a lot, too. I would go on long walks around my neighborhood and cry by myself. Our home is located in an area where the homes are stately and grand, many of them on the lake. I've always loved looking at pretty houses. This is how I spent the early days—just walking, crying, and talking to God.

The red brick classic Georgian home we purchased was a total and complete disaster. A major fixer-upper. Being in real estate, I knew that one is always supposed to buy the worst house in the best neighborhood, and that is exactly what we did. It felt overwhelming because it was a real wreck.

There was so much confusion during those first few weeks in our new surroundings. I would cry to anyone who would listen to me. I couldn't hold back—and these outbursts were embarrassing and unexpected. The guy came to hang our TVs…and I cried. The neighbor ladies asked me to lunch. "How is it is going?" they asked… I burst out in tears, "It's hard," I'd say. "My kids are having a hard time adjusting," that was the lie I was telling everyone. I couldn't come right out and say, "Oh, my husband and I moved our family down here so he could join a new oncology practice, and he feels like it was a mistake." I couldn't tell them that depression had hit Matthew like a ton of bricks. There was no way to explain that my once happy-go-lucky husband was going downhill, and quickly.

It started almost instantly—Matthew's depression and feeling of regret. I can't remember exactly the day he came home and said, "This move was career suicide. I feel like I am watching a slow car crash"—but it was soon after we'd arrived. *What the heck?* I thought to myself. Matthew had a tendency to be dramatic. I told him he needed to relax—that everyone has a hard time adjusting to a new job. Everyone says it takes at least a year to adjust and get familiar with new systems, new people, new everything. He had been with the same group for 16 years, so this was to be expected. But Matthew wasn't adjusting *at all*.

Matthew initially joined a bicycling club. This group met every Wednesday night. They cycled, then grabbed a beer at a local bar. We joined the yacht club. It is an adorable boating club on the lake, walkable from our home and so charming. I loved eating dinner on the veranda overlooking all of the beautiful boats parked in the marina. It was here that I met my first new friend, Missy. When Missy and I were chatting one night at dinner, I noticed that she wore a cross necklace, so I asked her where she attended church. She told me and gave me her phone number. She said that she had five boys and her husband was named Matt, too. I instantly loved Missy, there was just something about that girl. She invited my family to a party at her home over Labor Day weekend. This was very unexpected and very kind of this stranger to include us Midwesterners.

The party was fantastic! Missy and her Matt have a lovely home on the lake. We had drinks and dinner. Kids were playing in the pool and riding their jet skis on the lake. It was a festive evening, and I remember thinking to

myself, these Southerners really are something else! I remember thinking, *I love it here.* When the party was wind-
ing down, I looked over at Matthew; he just didn't look
like himself. His eyes weren't the same. There was a sadness in them that I'd never seen before. He was ready to
leave the party…before me, and that was a first. Matthew
Gall had always been the *last* one to leave a party.

One morning, a few days later, I was out walking our
dog Liberty when I met a gorgeous neighbor named
Cynda. She was so pretty, and I could tell she was fun. I
loved her Southern drawl. We got to chatting, and I explained how we'd just moved into the neighborhood. She
invited me to a "girls gathering" that she was hosting that
very evening at her house. I said I'd be there. When we
decided to move to the South, I knew I was going to have
to say yes to everything. Every chance I could get to meet
new people, I was going to take. I was 49 years old, and it
isn't like you're meeting new friends with your kids at
school or the park like we did when they were little.

Cynda and I became fast friends. I noticed instantly
that people in the South talk about their faith openly and
freely, which was foreign to me growing up in Minnesota.
I mean, these sorts of things were not openly discussed
with random strangers on the street. Cynda invited me to
a Bible study. I'd been attending church regularly since we
moved, but I didn't feel as though I'd found my home
church yet, so I was still church shopping.

Cynda handed me a little card. "I've never done this before," she said. "I've never invited anyone to a Bible study, but there are so many good ones!" I took the card, and sure enough there were. I picked, *It's Not Supposed to be This Way* by Lysa TerKeurst. Pretty much summed up my life at the time.

I came into the Bible study late; the study had started a few weeks earlier. But I read the book and got caught up. The book unveils author Lysa TerKeurst's heart amid shattering circumstances and explains how to live assured when life doesn't turn out like we expected. Tuesday mornings at 10 became the most important time of the week for me. I needed something to grasp onto. Matthew's new job was not what he expected. I kept saying, "Matthew—it's a job! Let's please quit and move back to Minnesota." He'd look around the house with a bewildered look in his eye and say, "But all of our stuff is here." I kept saying, "It's just stuff. I got it down here and I can get it back." It was like he couldn't comprehend it. He felt trapped and explained that it wouldn't be easy to go back to Minnesota because of the noncompete agreement in his old contract. Matthew was prevented from working within a fifty-mile radius of any of The Group's sites for one year. I suggested we move to our lake home where there was a great little hospital, and Matthew knew some of the doctors that worked there. He simply would not entertain the idea.

Matthew stopped sleeping a few weeks after we arrived in North Carolina. He'd always been the best sleeper, a good solid seven to eight hours a night, and now it was more like three or four max, if even. I am the earlier riser, and I was the one who woke up every morning and hit the gym. Half my day was already over by the time Matthew usually left for work. Not now. Everything had changed. I'd wake up, look over and see that he was awake staring at the ceiling. It was scary, and I was worried for him. As an oncologist, Matthew was dealing with life-and-death situations every day, and he needed to be sharp and alert for his patients.

It's now late October of 2019, and never in a million years would I have thought that my life could go from so good to so bad, so fast. Selling the house, doing everything, it all felt like "too much." Moving twice—half of our belongings wouldn't fit into our smaller home down south so those items had to go north to the lake. Everything else came here to North Carolina, paying the bills, trying to help Grady with his ongoing struggles, enrolling kids in school, working my real estate job, organizing every single detail of all five of our lives. It's all been me, alone, doing it all. Matthew has always been an excellent doctor and a wonderful provider. He took care of the lawn and would sometimes grill dinner—but everything else fell on my shoulders.

I've never been around a depressed person. It is not fun. He can't do anything anymore. Not the lawn, he won't grill or even go for a bike ride. I have to drag him to church. Matt doesn't drink anymore. Honestly, he loves beer so much, craft beers especially. Alcohol played a role in our life, and it did concern me at times, but now…nada. Zilch. No drinking at all. There is absolutely no joy, but I continue to try. I try encouraging words, I pray, I tell him what he has to do—but nothing happens.

I am here because of my kids, and I still love Matt, but he is not making it easy. I know that deep down he is a good person. He cares deeply, maybe too deeply. Is that possible? The good days seem to be over—and it is awful. Now I sit here, reading my morning devotionals and Bible verses, praying for a miracle. The silver lining for me coming to North Carolina was getting closer to God. I've met seven amazing women here. I know that I will continue to be in touch with them. I love them, yet I hardly know them.

My friend's statement the other day was telling, foreshadowing maybe. She said, "The one who is at the lowest for the longest period of time will eventually bring the other one down." I was a little offended and saddened, shown by my sobs on the phone to her. I thought to myself, Not me. *I've tried to get Matthew to spring into action, but honestly, I don't see that happening. We have three teenagers, not sure what I am going to do. He can't bring me down with him; our kids need their parents. I need to stay strong.*

I need to start making some decisions. My plan this week is to just get through the week. Matt has a meeting on Wednesday, and we speak to our life coach on Friday. I've hired our trusted life coach from Minneapolis. We're now paying the bill ourselves because it's important that we continue talking to him. If Matthew can't start networking, if he can't put an action plan in motion, I am going to start my plan:

1. *The house. Get information on what we could sell this home for. I need to meet with a local realtor.*

2. *Exit plan will come in June. We have to move back to Minnesota. I wish we could do this earlier, but the kids need to finish school. Matthew needs to give this practice four months' notice.*

3. *I'll get my real estate license back to an active status by then. We can live at my parents' house or at the lake.*

4. *I will, throughout these next seven months, continue to support Matthew. I honestly hope our marriage survives this. I need to lean in on my faith. Currently, he is not the same person that I married.*

Matt's problems seem to be deeply seated. I guess I never understood how much pressure he was under all the time. He loves his patients so much and is constantly talking about their care.

Chapter 4
Matthew's Worried

I knew Matthew took his vows to be a doctor and his Hippocratic oath very seriously. I wondered: *What is going on?* I know this wasn't what we thought it would be, but it seemed that the practice was thrilled to have Matthew onboard. I don't understand what the problem is.

I will continue to grow in God's love over the next few months. I'll continue attending church and going to Bible study, I will continue to learn and try to become a better person. I will try to worry less, control less, and talk less. I will look at myself and try to improve myself. I will dig deep. Matthew and I only wanted what was best for our kids. Matthew always wanted more, and wanted the best. We can't take the "stuff" with us when we die. We can't buy happiness. I've told him this a million times over. I want to move to the lake and live a simpler life.

I want happy kids and a good, uncomplicated life—that is what I desire. I want to enjoy quality time with my family and our friends. I need to also let go of the past and live in the present. I know I am far from perfect, but I also know I am amazingly strong, and like my dad always told me growing up, "You can do anything that you put your mind to." Matthew has always believed this, too.

I took wedding vows; both sets of our parents are still together. That gives me hope, as I never, ever thought I'd be divorced. Deep down, I don't want to be. But sadly, I cannot change Matthew. Only he can do that. I've always viewed him as a go-getter, a fighter, but now as he suffers, and is paralyzed with regret and fear—I am not so sure. I am very confused. I guess time will tell. I'm in it for better or worse, as of now. I will try and hold my head high through this deep valley. I will continue to support him, but he needs to fight his own battle, too—I cannot do it for him. As I stumble through the days ahead, I may remember this Bible verse:

"For I know the plans I have for you, declares the Lord, plans to prosper you and not harm you, plans to give you hope and a future." – Jeremiah 29:11.

Trying to calm myself, I repeat this over and over:
I'm not anxious, I'm calm.
> **Celebrate the Lord**
> **Ask for everything**
> **Leave the problems with Him**
> **Meditate in all good things**

I honestly can't believe this is my life right now, it is the end of October 2019. I feel numb, sad, and oh-so scared about our future. On the other hand, I feel safe, like this will all work out, that we have to go through the process and trust the Lord. Matthew is getting worse with his depression. He is very negative, and I'm not sure how I can help anymore. I am afraid that something bad will happen to him, and I'm not sure he can take the pressure much more. I've made a plan:

Matthew must:

1. Write a letter to The Group, asking for his job back in Minnesota.
2. Call a recruiter and start looking for a new position, just in case they won't give Matthew his old job back.
3. Call the hospital system at the clinic up north by our lake home.
4. Talk with the life coach.
5. Talk with our lawyer friend.

That is all happening within the next two days. I need to move forward, and I can't look back.

What I am grateful for today:

- The people I've met in North Carolina, so many good people
- My Bible study at church. Who would have thought?
- The sermons that are always spot on

◎ *Healthy kids. I love them so much, and I pray that they don't hate us*

I want to be back in Minnesota by next summer. Everything will fall into place as it usually seems to do. I am praying for a miracle—that The Group leaders in Minnesota will take Matthew back. We need a miracle God, please help us.

It's early November, and I still can't believe this is my life right now. Things have taken a turn for the worse, as if that is even possible. Matthew says he feels as if he's "imploding." He keeps saying that word over and over. I can't help but feel responsible. We thought this move was going to be great for everyone. Matt said he needed a fresh start. I have so much anxiety, my heart is always racing and my palms are sweaty. I've never experienced this before. Matthew's college buddy is a well-respected lawyer. They spoke and Matthew told him that he feels like a fool. The lawyer friend said, "Matthew, this move was a swing and a miss." However, Matthew is more concerned about caring for his patients properly than taking care of himself.

We spoke to the life coach on the phone Friday. He said that we have time to figure things out, but I really don't feel that way. He hasn't actually seen Matthew—who now physically looks different. I cannot eat, I cannot sleep, and I am worried about the kids. Sophie does not want to play volleyball right now, and Gavin never wants to be home. Grady got a job, and I am grateful because it is keeping him out of trouble.

Matt's older brother Chris and wife Diane will be here the next weekend, and I fear that our sadness will rain on their parade. They are excited to move here. I feel strongly that we need to get back to Minnesota so Matt can practice medicine the way he is accustomed to. I know it will be difficult to move back, as our old home is not ours anymore. How could we have been so naïve? We were trusting, optimistic, hopeful, and now our lives are in disarray. If only, if only, if only...we had talked to people about our fears before we left. If only we had thought things through more. But no, we ran—so Matt could have a fresh start, and I ran because I thought it would help Grady. How does one bounce back from such a serious mistake? I need to let Matthew figure some of this out on his own, too. I need to say less. But I'm scared, God. I know I need to trust you more, but I'm so scared.

Things are not getting any easier here. I hate this sinking-ship feeling. I can look forward, but Matt cannot. He ruminates about the old house, and his old job. I fear he will never be the same again. It's like watching a slow death of someone you love and adore. I'm sick for him, sick for us, sick for our family. Matt is such an amazing guy, but he is not doing himself or any of us favors. Not sure how to move forward. I feel nauseated—I want my old life back.

Trying to remain positive, but it's been a hard day. Not going to lie—Matthew won't do any of the things he used to love to do. He won't grill, he used to salivate just talking about meat products. He won't mow the lawn, or even go on a walk with me. It's like he's shutting down. His perfectionism seems to be getting worse, and he is not sleeping at all. I guess I was stupid to think I'd be free from any problems. My life was pretty darn easy up until Grady's freshman year. I wish I'd been a better mom. Maybe if I would've paid closer attention, Grady never would've been bullied.

I'm sad, and discouraged, and this will be my first Thanksgiving away from home. I'm not sure that I'll be able to decorate for Christmas. I'm upset today thinking about all of this. I wanted my kids to have a normal, happy childhood, but I fear we've ruined it for them. I'm frightened right now because I don't know what the future holds. I don't know how to act because I truly don't feel like myself. But maybe all of this uncomfortableness is preparing me to be a better version of myself—a kinder, more empathetic Christian who loves people and can help people? What if God is preparing Matthew for the same? What if working here in North Carolina is going to make him a better doctor? Maybe, just maybe, this will turn out okay. Or maybe it won't. I need to trust the Lord; I am not in control. Please Lord, take away my fear and anxiety for today. Help me become a better human being.

"Do not be anxious about anything, but in every situation, by prayer and petition with thanksgiving, present your requests to God." – Philippians 4:6

I am trying to believe in this verse and I have it on repeat in my brain, but my heart is racing. I'm thinking about what bad things could happen if Matthew is unable to work. Being a doctor means everything to him. His patients mean the world to him, and he loves being a doctor more than anything. I don't know what we were thinking. I should have known better that he is a creature of habit. Now we are here, and he hates it with an absolute passion. I am scared for him. He has the weight of the world on his shoulders. I pray he doesn't harm himself. I've had awful thoughts of death and dying lately. I can't shake them. I need to be grateful for all that we have. I truly believe Matt needs to get out of this job and get back to Minnesota.

Dear God, let something go in Matthew's favor, maybe get the job up at the lake if it is to be, may we all get back to Minnesota, may Grady please pass math and graduate on time so he can go out on his own, go to college, and get a job. Oh Lord, I pray for these things. You have been so good to me in the past, and I now need you more than ever.

The most incredible thing happened at Bible study today. First of all, the testimony was unbelievable. The woman spoke of how we are all traveling through a valley—all of us at different times and at different speeds, so to say. This sweet-natured, red-headed woman was standing on the stage with a Bible in her hand and told us of the horrific journey her family has been through. In 2018, she lost her three-year-old daughter—and her brother, was charged with involuntary manslaughter of her daughter. How this beautiful mother, wife, daughter, and sister was able to get up on stage and share her story, I'll never know. Her problems make my problems seem so insignificant. She talked about Psalm 23:4: "Even though I walk through the darkest valley, I will fear no evil, for you are with me; your rod and your staff, they comfort me." And then she went on to talk about the lilies of the valley. It was an amazing testimony of her faith in God, her strength to persevere. I was speechless.

Today was about praying with others, and our leader encouraged us to go get a prayer from the women who were standing. I was drawn to this petite Black woman with short curly hair. I wanted to pray with her for some reason. But I had to wait. Another person was already with her. Out of the blue, a super kind young woman asked if she could pray with me, and I said yes. She asked what I needed help with, and I said we'd recently moved for a new job for my husband. She said a lovely prayer over our finances, prayed for patience, and for Matthew to be able to hear the Lord. I was a little bummed because, while wonderful, she wasn't who I initially wanted to pray with. That was okay, and I went back to my seat. We sang a hymn and went to class.

Class was perfect as usual, and it was what I needed. Amanda, my new friend, is utterly amazing. She is very pretty, with beautiful skin and dark hair, she's petite, wears glasses, and has a fabulous soul. I adore her. I sit next to her and Lucy in every class. We read a lot of scripture, and she told us to pray. Again, we were asked to pray with others, "When two or more are gathered," which is something that my mother always told me. *Again, she encouraged us to pray with the women that were standing. And guess what? There was the petite Black lady, waiting there for me. She asked my desires and I told her prayers for my husband. She asked if he was a believer. "Yes," I said. She asked his name. "Matthew. Oh, a child of God." "Yes," I said. She grabbed my hands and asked for God to speak through her. She shuddered and mumbled a little, and I felt the power within her.*

She told me to tell Matthew that he should not have any regrets. She said God brought us here for a reason. She said he is a caring soul, a kind soul, a good man. She said God told her to tell him to be patient, and that everything would be okay. She told me to tell him to pray. She shuddered and mumbled some more, and I simply sobbed. She was holding my hands, so I couldn't even wipe the snot and the tears that were dripping down my face. She gave me the best hug ever. I went back to my table where others were praying. I cried some more, prayed some more. And then, Judy, who obviously recently had a breast removed (you could visibly see the bandages, and I saw the breast cancer ribbon bracelet she was wearing) asked me if I wanted a hug. "Yes," I said. And she hugged me. There I was in my blue blazer with gold buttons, gold watch, and tight jeans, looking pretty good—minus the red splotchy face, getting a bear hug from a complete stranger. It was a moving morning, to say the least. The petite Black woman then came to my table and handed me a note for Matthew. It says this:

To Matthew:
There are no mountains that can stop him.
He has the power and the authority to
block the enemy from obstructing his path.
We bind the enemy for speaking negative
words to him.
        Love and blessings.

She didn't sign it, and I still do not know her name. She is a saint in my eyes.

God brought us here for a reason—I know I needed to get closer to Him. I was off track. I'm such a "fixer," a worrier, a "what if" type of person. I've been worried about the kids, about Matt, about the job. I cannot be anxious. I have always been very blessed. Here, we have been planning to run back to Minnesota, but what if we are not supposed to? What if we are to be right here, right now, for a reason? What if this house will get remodeled? What if good comes out of this? What if I'm prepared to go to heaven? What if Matthew becomes a better person, a better doctor? Why do I look only at the bad possibilities? I'm just so confused; life feels utterly chaotic.

I do have faith in the Lord—that He will watch over us. Why have I been this blessed? Why would Matt and I think that we wouldn't have to walk through a valley of our own? I can beat myself up for sending my kids to private school, for building the house in Minnesota, for everything—the past is the past, and I'm here now. I'm here now for a reason.

I've met amazing, wonderful, incredible friends here. I've found God to be all around me. I've gotten closer to my parents by being away from them. I know that I need to concentrate on relationships, God, my kids, my family, and not being perfect. The "perfect" house is gone. We are in a valley of uncertainty, and the only way out is to go through it. There is a glimmer of light—and I know it will grow brighter as God continues to reveal His plan to us. He is an amazing God, and I am blessed to get to know Him better.

Chapter 5
Family Visits

November 11, 2019. *Matt's older brother Chris, his wife Diane, and my nephew, Andrew, 19, arrived from Wisconsin late last night. They are moving here to North Carolina, which is super. We were really looking forward to living close to each other; however Matthew now feels a tremendous amount of guilt about it. I've be confiding in my sister-in-law Diane that things aren't going well for us. It is wonderful to have them here, and I'm hoping it'll be good for Matthew, too.*

Diane had previously been a social worker—and she was shocked at the way Matthew physically looked. There is a vacancy in his eyes. His tone is flat. We've both lost weight. We are so exhausted neither of us looks good. Diane pleaded with Matthew to get on an anti-depressant. He kept saying he couldn't because of the side effects, and that he didn't want to lose his medical license.

I think to myself, Why would a doctor lose his medical license for getting treatment? *But I guess Matt would know—he's the doctor.*

Yesterday was beautiful. I took Liberty to the park for a long walk, but I'm frightened Lord, even though you tell me not to be. Thoughts about death have been creeping into my mind, and I try to fight them back, and then I think that maybe I am being prepared for something bad to happen. I hope and pray that things do not get worse for us. Matthew is in such a state, and I don't know how he is dealing with the pressure and stress, but he is. Barely. Everything regarding our future is hanging in the balance.

At this point, I want to go back to Minnesota as soon as possible, even as hard as it will be without my beautiful house there. I don't know why we gave it all up based on what ifs, but we did. I was trying to save everyone—Matthew and Grady— and I fear it was a terrible mistake. God put me here to get closer to Him, that I know, but I have to ask, At what cost, God? I don't even feel like myself at all. I'm a shell of my former self, and I miss parts of the old me, like my job, waking up every morning feeling secure. I have none of that here. I have to take two melatonin pills every night to help me fall asleep, and it's awful. I miss my routine, my parents, my house, planning vacations, dinner with neighbors, short drives to the lake house, lunch with the girls, and my book club. I miss it all. We gave it all away. And for this? At what cost, God?

I've always tried to do the right thing. I'm so far from perfect, but I feel very tortured right now. This kitchen is awful, the bathrooms are ugly, and the backyard is overgrown. Everything seems to be a mess. Everything is overwhelming. And yet, I have to be patient and wait. Thessalonians 5:14: "And we urge you, brothers and sisters, warn those who are idle and disruptive, encourage the disheartened, help the weak, be patient with everyone." It is painful, but it's what I will do.

I trust in the Lord, I believe in God, I know that we are currently going through the valley—I know that we will get through it and not be stuck in it. I know God loves me and my family. I pray all the time for Matthew. He can be difficult some days, but he is also kind and caring, and I know that he is a really good, compassionate doctor. But oh Lord, for today, I want my old life back. I never let my mind go there like Matt does, but today I really miss my old life. I wish I'd remembered the quotation that my mom talked about. Maybe then I wouldn't have been so irritated with Matthew in the past. Something along the lines of this: the way to love is to always remember and realize that it might be lost.

Philippians 4:6-7. "Do not be anxious about anything, but in every situation, by prayer and petition, with thanksgiving, present your requests to God. And the peace of God, which transcends all understanding, will guard your hearts and your minds in Christ Jesus." I still have this verse on repeat in my brain.

November 14, 2019 – Gavin is 15 today! Seriously, where does the time go? I wish Gavin were 100 percent happy. He misses home and all of his friends. I wish I could take all of his pain away. This move has been rough on him. He's so much like Matt. We are going out for pizza tonight. He gets to go to Young Life Camp with his new buddies this weekend, and I am happy he has something to look forward to because I think he will have a blast.

I had a really tough day two days ago. I broke down on the phone with Megan, my best friend since the second grade. I was extremely tired, and I lost it. Matthew's behavior really freaks me out. He is simply not himself. He worries about patient care, he's using words like "career suicide" and "exposed," he dreams about death and a "slow car crash." This is awful to hear day after day. He keeps repeating that we are going to lose everything. This feels chaotic. We are all urging him to get help, get on anti-depressants, but he won't. I'm going the tough-love route and told him he needs to talk and confide in someone else if he's not going to help himself. I have three kids to take care of. I hope God isn't preparing me for his death. I pray he listens to me and gets the help he needs.

Grady is smoking pot again, and I'm devastated. He said he doesn't think he's college material. Thinking about it makes me tear up. I hope he wakes up and decides to go to college in the fall. As a friend recently said to me, "Only Grady can change Grady. Maybe someday he'll get sick and tired of being sick and tired." One can only pray. He's such a beautiful boy who has a beautiful soul. I wish he could see this. I guess that's true for all of us. I'm trying to help Matthew, trying to get him to change, but he is stuck. I hope he will snap out of it. He's Matthew Gall after all! He's strong and smart and has much to live for. Ugh, he won't listen to me. I'm off to Bible study, it's the only thing I have to look forward to. I love these women.

Went to see the movie Ford vs. Ferrari *last night with Matthew, Chris, and Diane. We grabbed a drink afterward. I love North Carolina. Unfortunately, Matthew only talks about work. On Friday, I asked him to please take the weekend off from thinking about work, his regrets, and his past, but he can't seem to do that. I truly don't know how I am functioning right now. It must be my unwavering faith in God who has continued to provide for us. Yes, we have been blessed. We've always had everything we needed, but now I can't picture my future. My readings are telling me to have patience and perseverance. How long do I wait, Lord?*

Ugh, back in Minnesota, Matthew said he couldn't go on under "this much scrutiny," and he was under pressure—declining reimbursements, threats from the hospital to buy out The Group, long hours, and that terrifying death threat. Those damn surveys that raised complaints. Matthew felt those stemmed mostly from when he was rushed. But then again, he is allotted only a certain time to see patients. And he is paid partly on production…it's a vicious cycle. He did great for a while, but I guess physician burnout is truly real. I never understood that. It's caught up with him, and now I'm not sure he can handle the

pressure of this change. Underneath his flaws, which I am re-
minded that we all have—I know Matthew is a good, caring
soul, and a fantastic doctor. Matt loves his family, he loves me,
but he is undeniably a tortured soul right now. It's painful to
watch, and painful to be a part of it. I keep telling myself that we
are going through the valley right now, and it will not be like
this forever.

Psalm 23:1-6 "The Lord is my shepherd; I lack nothing. He
makes me to lie down in green pastures, he leads me beside quiet
waters, he refreshes my soul. He guides me along the right paths
for his name's sake. Even though I walk through the darkest val-
ley, I will fear no evil, for you are with me; your rod and your
staff, they comfort me. You prepare a table before me in the pres-
ence of my enemies. You anoint my head with oil; my cup over-
flows. Surely your goodness and love will follow me all the days
of my life, and I will dwell in the house of the Lord forever."

November 18th is a dreary morning here. I started in prayer
and doing a workout to my Jesus music. It's all I listen to now.
I didn't know this music even existed when I lived in Minnesota.
I find it so hopeful and inspirational. But for whatever reason, I
can't shake this feeling of death surrounding Matthew. I pray
my gut is wrong. He is so tortured right now, and we are in a
wilderness of uncertainty. I have no idea where he is on his faith
journey. I'm not his judge, I wish he could see what I see—that
he can get through this. I see two visions: happiness, it will be a

different happiness in Minnesota. And the other, I have this sinking feeling of his death. He's so dramatic, I hope his feeling of "mental illness" and a "fatal" mistake are wrong. I pray that he can pull through this. I honestly do not know, I am so confused. I'm praying, praying, praying all the time to take the sickness out of his brain. He is so sad, so full of anxiety and depression. It's hard to bring happiness and joy into the house when he is here. Gavin is now struggling, too. I love them all so much, but I feel as though our life is falling apart.

A guy friended me on Facebook. I went to high school with him, but didn't know him. He's an anesthesiologist in Minneapolis. I accepted his request while lying in bed next to Matthew. His post: He's going to give a talk on physician suicide. I think to myself , What the heck—you mean this is a thing? *I couldn't stop shaking, I leaned over and asked Matthew, who was staring at the ceiling, "Did you know that doctors kill themselves a lot?" I mean I can't believe it, they are doctors. This is a thing? Matthew simply nodded. He knows this. Oh my God, my heart is sinking.*

Yesterday was the brunch at church celebrating the final Bible study of this season. I almost didn't go, but am happy I did. Oh my, the testimonies were unbelievable. For example: The Asian lady whose parents beat her, and she ended up taking care of them on their death bed. The beautiful girl who was in jail for drugs and alcohol—and she found Jesus and is forgiven and redeemed. The white-haired lady with the glasses, curls, and unforgettable giggle who talked about the hymn class. It was wonderful to be surrounded by such amazing, strong, beautiful women. We all have something to deal with in our lives, and yet we can overcome.

It was also a very hard day, as Matt told me it was "D" day. I don't understand what that means but he's freaking me out. I was standing in the powder bathroom, and he came sliding down the hallway in his socks and his hair was all messy. He was suddenly in the mirror behind me. He said, "It's D-day." I started shaking. He is scaring me. My heart is constantly racing. He talked about "career suicide" again; he keeps saying we are going to lose everything. I was literally petrified all day. It's terrible living like this, not knowing what is happening to my husband. It was my girlfriend Ann's birthday, and all I could think about was the fact that my life is going to look very different a year from now. God has been good to me, and He will continue to be as long as I follow Him and be thankful.

I finished my book as I lay on my bed yesterday, tired, sad, and worried. I then remembered to download the book that Joy mentioned at Bible study the other day, One Thousand Gifts *by Ann Voskamp. By page 30, I was hooked, so I continue my list of Things to Be Grateful For.*

- ◎ *Grady's smile*
- ◎ *Walking Liberty in the sunshine*
- ◎ *Making dinner for all five of us*
- ◎ *The precious moments in the car with the kids*
- ◎ *Matthew is breathing; he is alive*

- *Matthew has a job and an income*
- *Matthew's parents arrive in three days*
- *My mother's texts telling me she loves me*
- *An invitation to dinner with Jennifer and her husband*
- *Love in the middle of the night*

I spoke to my hairdresser yesterday. She thinks we came here to save Grady. I think so, too.

- *New friends who invite us to socialize*
- *Nephew Andrew for fixing my car, I think my car is a lemon*
- *Our lawyer friend for texting Matthew encouraging words*
- *Laundry to keep me busy...I used to loathe doing the laundry*
- *Time spent alone with Sophie*

I cannot control my future. I cannot control Matthew or Grady or anyone for that matter. But I can control me and my thoughts, my journey and my reactions. God has given us exactly what we need, and much more. Three healthy and beautiful (inside and out) children. Parents that are alive and still together. Awesome brothers and sisters-in-laws. Really, who could ask for anything more? We have an abundance of good friends. We have been blessed with good health, and I'm now down 20 pounds. This is a good weight for me, physically in that regard, I feel fantastic, but I am tired beyond belief. I only wish Matt could see and appreciate all of the gifts and blessings that we have. I love my life and wish Matthew could love his too. I'll keep working on him. I'll keep talking to God and praying. I pray that something good happens for him soon.

- *Walking outside without a coat on November 22*
- *A car that works*
- *My trusted financial advisor, who is also my confidant and good friend*
- *My running shoes; workouts are currently a breeze*

Last night we had dinner at the country club with Shelly and her husband. They could become great friends if our life was normal. I met Shelly at a party where we chatted briefly, but then ran into her at the grocery store a few days later. She asked us to dinner. That's what I love about the South, people ask you to do things and really mean it. It's not like that in Minnesota. If Matthew were himself, maybe we'd have a shot at a new, full social life here. But right now, I feel as though I am keeping a secret. How can I share with people that my brilliant doctor husband is depressed? He's supposed to be building a new practice, after all.

At three in the morning, Matthew wakes up in a cold sweat, worried about his patients and about "a slow car crash." I am petrified and I can no longer sleep. He wakes me up all the time, and I am angry with him. Why can't he snap out of this? Why won't he get help? Our dear friend, Dr. Foley from Minnesota, has been telling him to see a psychiatrist, but Matt refused. I'm not sure what to do at this point. I've always believed in him, so I can't lose hope now.

Matthew's parents come to visit on Monday, and I need to tell them everything—maybe they can help. In the midst of Matt's nighttime worry session, he asked that I put back the bathroom light I had removed. What the heck? I do think he's mentally ill, Lord. The OCD, the perfectionism and worry has crept into all areas in his life. He complains about the garage being a mess. We have newly epoxied floors, new garage doors, and empty shelves. Nothing is a mess or out of order. This house is far from perfect, but it is organized and clean. I am realizing that he is really sick. Why won't he get help? He thinks he'll lose his medical license. Is this true? I don't know what to believe.

I'm staring at a picture of the kids on a vacation in Costa Rica, thinking of how great my life used to be. I think about Matt on vacation and remember him always bringing his New England Journals of Medicine. *One could never keep up with all of those magazines he received weekly in the mail. Even while on vacation, he felt the need to keep up by reading those journals.*

- ◎ *Memories of Costa Rica*
- ◎ *Memories of a beautiful trip to St. Kitts*
- ◎ *Ski vacations in Beaver Creek*
- ◎ *Lunch with a new friend last week*
- ◎ *Coffee and creamer*

- Jesus Calling *book*
- Deserts in the Stream *book*
- *Two days until Matt's parents come*

I'm a planner, Lord, and I know I'm being taught a lesson. I need to be patient and live in the present, but I am thinking about the next steps for my kids, whether to finish school here or go back to Minnesota.

- *Delta flight on December 21st that will get us back to Minnesota*
- *Sweet Liberty sleeping in her pink bed*
- *All of my children sleeping safely in their beds*
- *My broken kitchen lamp still lights up my desk so I can write*
- *God, I'm grateful for my parents*
- *My friends, I'm blessed to have so many*

It's Saturday, Lord, and I used to love Saturdays. Sadly, I don't anymore. I don't want to be around Matthew's negativity. I've talked and talked, supported, uplifted, cheered, and sang his praises, but he doesn't listen to me. I fear he is weak. Matt Gall and weak are two words that before, I never thought I'd use in the same sentence. I remember he once told Grady not to use his depression as a crutch and that suicide was for cowards. This makes me angry.

I will be 50 years old in two months. This is not how I pictured my life to be. I'm trusting the Lord right now and thanking Him for these hard times because I know when we get through them that there will be glory and light on the other side. I do need to figure out what the other side and the next 50 years will look like. Then again, I'm not in control. He is. Dear Lord, I thank you for these three beautiful sleeping children. I thank you for this house, and my parents, and for cars that work. We have food and shelter. I am so lucky. I thank you, Lord, for loving me. I thank you for providing for me and blessing my life a thousand times over. God wastes nothing. Romans 8:31: "What, then, shall we say in response to these things? If God is for us, who can be against us?"

- *Raindrops that fit my mood*
- *Knowing God will bring the sunshine back tomorrow*
- *New friend Lisa for inviting me to the college talk at the high school*
- *Fall colors and leaves changing*
- *A quiet afternoon*
- *Freshly polished fingernails*
- *A closet full of clothes*
- *Knowing everything I need for today, I have*

Chapter 6

Matthew is Given Anti-Depressants

D r. Foley prescribed anti-depressants for Matthew yesterday. Ambien, too. He won't take them. I went to church in the rain by myself last night. Oh, how Saturday nights have changed.

- My cozy bed, and my numerous pillows
- Sound of Matt's sleep-apnea machine working next to me
- Matthew actually smiled last night
- Texts from my Minnesota friends
- Feeling rested. Nothing better than a good night's sleep
- A full day planned
- Grady waking me up and giving me a hug
- Not feeling anxious
- Knowing everything I need for today, I have. (I said this over and over to myself)

I'm going to church this morning. Churches are about the people, and the people at my church are amazing. My Bible study ladies, even Joe the contractor that came over to give me a quote the other day, attends our church. His wife was my leader in Bible study. She beat cancer. Amanda, Cynda, and Lucy whom I recently met all go to same church, which feels like a home church to me. Maybe God has Matthew's medical license held up in Minnesota so he can go back to The Group when they need him? It's hard to dream this big and ask for such a miracle…but with God, anything is possible.

◉ *Knowing it isn't always going to be this way*

I've led such a blessed life, I have three beautiful kids and a husband that truly loves me. We not only have a nice home, but I have clothes in my closet and food in the pantry, so of course I'm due a trial. As I look around, I realize that everyone has trials—life is a valley, and we're going through it, and I do believe we will forever be changed for the better after this is over. I have faith in God.

◉ *Strong legs to run*
◉ *Neighbors that know your name*
◉ *Colors changing on the crunchy leaves*
◉ *Accepting the mystery of life*
◉ *God transforming deep inside me*
◉ *Dreams of helping homeless veterans*
◉ *Clearer direction day by day*

- *Thoughts of home*
- *Words that come to us to help us heal*
- *Big windows that help the light shine in*
- *Any church and every church*
- *Unexpected smell of lilies in the valley*
- *Airplanes to bring family closer*
- *Another breath*
- *Being able to confide in Angie, who is a physician and is trying to help us*
- *Dawn rises through the darkness*

It's November 25, and it's not a good day. Matthew is still freaking out. My heart is racing, and I keep praying he doesn't do something stupid. His parents just landed, but Matthew is not happy about his parents being here, which is strange. He's usually extremely excited to see his parents. Diane is getting them from the airport, then they're coming over. I'm going to tell them everything, a complete and total download of what's been going on. We've never told them about all of the issues and pressures Matt had been facing. I talked to Dr. Foley this morning, and again he said that Matthew needs to see a psychiatrist, take the anti-depressant, and he also needs to exercise and sleep. I can't get him to do any of these things. It's so very frustrating.

Matt didn't take his medications today. I don't think he slept much last night. He woke me up at 1:51 a.m. worrying about Sophie. Everything is a mess. I was hoping Matt could hold on until December 27—to make it back home to Minnesota, and I could take him to the lake house where he could see how much he has to fight for. I don't think he can stay at this job much longer, and I don't know what to do. Lord, I need help, I really need help. I'm scared beyond belief. I understand that Matt is sick…and he has no hope.

Matt's parents have landed, and I'm waiting for Di to text me. Then they will come over for the whole download. How did this become my life? I did talk to Matthew, and he was getting through his day but said he was having trouble with his treatment plans. This is unlike him, and I don't want to downplay anything he says. He really has me worked up now that I'm thinking we are going to lose everything. We are not, I refuse to let that happen. I will fight for the family that I love so much. Matthew said, "I don't think I can be a doctor anymore." What the heck?!?! "Okay," I said, "Matt, you're super smart, I know you can figure out something else to do. This is a job, and there are many of them out there." I know if he could sleep for a good solid week or two, he'd be able to think more clearly. His brain — it's not functioning right.

At 7:30 this morning, I had a meeting with Grady, his counselor, and his math teacher. Oh, that was about as much fun as poking a needle in my eye. Grady told his teacher that she was "rude." I wanted to crawl under her desk and hide. I had to apologize profusely. Grady needs to pass math — he needs to keep his eye on the prize. I need Grady to graduate on June 11th so that on June 12th, we can head back to Minnesota. I wonder what my life will look like in a year, oh Lord, please let it look better, *let us be in a happier place. I want to be back in Minnesota and have Matthew back at The Group. One can dream, can't they? Please Lord, deliver us from the evil we are facing right now. I have to do something nice for this math teacher.*

Richard with pest control is here. He has a wonderful smile, and I like talking to him. I pretend I'm living a normal life. Shelly is so nice, she asked us for dinner at the club again on December 6, but I turned her down. I'm turning friends down left and right. It makes me sad because if Matthew were happy at work, everything could have fallen into place. My heart is broken, but my heart is strong. I will survive this. I will, and my hope is that Matthew will, too.

- *Matt's parents*
- *Chris, his brother*
- *Diane, my sister-in-law*
- *Grady's text to me after our meeting at school: "Thank you for helping me out. I know I don't always appreciate it, but I do. I know you want the best for me, so thank u." My reply: "I love you, Grady. You stole my heart the minute I laid eyes on you. I know you can do this. Thanks for the text, it means more to me than you'll ever know."*

Matt's parents will be here any minute.

Now it's 3:45 p.m., and Matt's parents, and Chris and Diane just left. They were awesome and very helpful, and I am grateful and relieved that they are here. They agree Matthew needs a psychiatrist, and he needs to take these medications that Dr. Foley prescribed. Matt can be quite melodramatic, I just don't know what to do anymore, I don't know what to believe. I hope and pray he can get through this. I can't let my mind go to bad places either. I need to stay positive, but this is really awful. We are going to talk to Matt when he gets home tonight.

At 5:30, Matthew's parents, Chris, Di, and I spoke to Matthew about the fact that he needs help. He needs to listen to us. Sitting in our living room, Matthew kept saying something to the effect of, "I can't take medication because of the side effects. I could lose my medical license." Is this true? I have no clue. He's said that to me more than once already.

Matt's Dad, Bruce, confided in us all that he'd been through something similar after his mom died. He couldn't sleep and had to be hospitalized. Does depression run in families? Maybe so, I know very little about this subject. Matthew has a vacant look in his eyes. We talked for at least an hour. Bruce was really in his face trying to get through to him. Matt sat by Elaine, his mom, who he dearly loves. He told her he loved her. Poor Elaine recently lost her sister to cancer, and I don't think that Matthew's mental illness is clear to her. Thank God for Auntie Diane. She has been a voice of reason for us all. Will Matt lose his medical license? I don't know. His whole identity is wrapped up into being a doctor. He knew that's what he wanted to do from the age of three. I truly don't know anything anymore. I am exhausted. We all agreed he needs to quit this job. January 1st, he will give his four-months' notice. Oh my gosh, it's so long, and he has a noncompete contract here in North Carolina, too! These noncompete clauses are adding to Matt's stress because he feels trapped. We can live at the lake house in Minnesota, or I'll stay here in North Carolina with the kids to finish school. I don't know, but we will figure it out.

Chris and my father-in-law Bruce took all of the guns out of our house. I knew we had guns, and Matthew had been carrying one to work in Minnesota. The boys always liked to go trap shooting. The boys are trained in gun safety. Matthew had respect for guns. My dad is a duck hunter, and while Matthew was not a hunter, he had several guns that had been gifts from both our dads. Matthew loved to go to the gun range and shoot.

Matthew was lying on the bed afterward, staring at the ceiling. He muttered, "They took my guns…" I simply said, "Matthew, this is temporary until you get better." I don't understand him, I can't seem to reach him. If he'd listen to us and get some sleep, he'd be able to think much clearer.

- ◎ *Parents – I am happy my mom is alive, and just a phone call away*
- ◎ *Sunshine, as it makes my days bearable*
- ◎ *Meals from Costco*
- ◎ *Walks with my darling friend Dawn*
- ◎ *The ability to write my words on paper*

On November 26. Please God, let Matthew make it to the next month—he'll be back home in Minnesota a month from tomorrow. We have a plan. Quit this job January 2, home by the end of May. God, please help me with my anxiety and worry. You've always blessed me and taken care of me and my family. I pray that the plan works. Dr. Foley has been amazing. Matt refused to take his medication today, but I made him. This is awful to watch and live through. I asked Matt if he took the pill. I made him open his mouth; the pill was sitting on his tongue. I made him swallow it. What the heck? *I think to myself. I'm scared. Our life coach is out of town. Good psychiatrists are difficult to find, but I need to quickly find one for Matthew. I can't believe this is my life.*

◎ *Deep talks with Sophie*
◎ *Eye-lash appointments*
◎ *Walks with Liberty*

Matt took an Ambien last night, but he slept for only four hours. He is nervous about making a mistake at work. He has never ever been fearful of making a mistake. I was hoping he could hang on until January 2, and then quit, but I'm not sure he is going to be able to. Nephew Andrew told my kids about the "intervention" we had with Matthew, so I had to explain to them a bit about what is going on. I have been trying to hide his depression from everyone, including our children, which hasn't been easy. I have everything I need for today, and I am grateful that Matt's parents are here.

Chapter 7

Thanksgiving – the Day Everything Changed

Matthew was out of his mind, so sad, and he hadn't slept. I wanted to take him to the hospital, but he wouldn't get in the car. He didn't want to go. He was so strong-willed. I'm mad because he could have gotten help. He was helpless and without hope, and he refused to help himself. Why?

Exhausted, I told Matt to get in the car. It was early on Thanksgiving Day, and I wanted to get him to the hospital where he could get some sleep. He got dressed so I could take him to the hospital downtown. He was wearing his glasses, blue sweat pants, white t-shirt, and grey puffy vest. He told me that he hated that hospital, but he finally agreed to go. He looked at me and said, "You're going to get married again." I yelled back, "MATTHEW! GET IN THE CAR NOW!"

I grabbed my purse and phone and wrote a note to the children telling them I was taking Dad to the hospital and that we'd be back. Matt was taking forever to come to the garage. It was *pitch black outside, what time was it? 5 a.m.? 6 a.m.? I have no idea. I went to look for Matthew inside the house. I walked back inside our dark house. I was whispering, "Matthew…Matthew." I noticed the door to the backyard was unlocked, and it's always locked. I opened the door to the backyard. "Matthew, are you there? You're scaring me," I whispered. It was so dark outside that I couldn't see anything. But I could hear movement in the bushes. I told him to get in the car, but he wouldn't come out of the bushes. The whole backyard is like a forest surrounding an old decrepit stone hot tub. I went to the car to get my phone, and I called 911. I came back to the door to tell Matt that I called 911. He asked, "Will there be sirens?" I said, "What? What in the heck are you talking about, Matthew?!?!" I was so confused, and my heart was racing at a million beats per second. I said, "I don't know Matthew, please get in the car because you're scaring me."*

I told the 911 operator on the phone that my husband was suicidal. She asked me, "Do you have any weapons in the house?" "NO! My brother-in-law and father-in-law took them all the other night." Or so I thought. I went back into the garage to close my car door, which I had left open, and while on the phone with 911, it was then that I heard the gun shot — Matthew had shot himself.

◎ *I'm thankful for the local police*

Oh my gosh, it seemed like it took forever for the police to get there, but I think it was really maybe like five minutes. They were very nice. Oh no…I don't know why Matthew had to do that. We had a plan to go back to Minnesota to go to the lake, and I told him our kids were going to fish off the dock with their kids. It was all he ever wanted. He loved that lake home. He loved me and the kids.

My life has been changed forever. It was Thanksgiving, for the love of God. The kids, me, the police. Talking, talking, talking, I couldn't stop. I kept asking, "Who will take the kids tubing?" Why was I repeating this question over and over? I asked one police officer if Matthew was really dead. He told me, "Yes"—it was true. I grabbed him, "No! He helps people like you, sir. Doctors kill themselves a lot. I didn't know that before. I wanted him to get better. I thought one day he'd simply snap out of it." I fell to the floor in this officer's arms. He held my head in his lap. I saw the tears in his eyes, too. I'll never forget him.

I called Diane, and they came over with Matthew's parents. The pastor and another sweet church member showed up. It was very early, on Thanksgiving Day, I couldn't believe they were here praying with me and the kids. We all sat at the kitchen table, just staring at each other in shock. My mind was racing. Oh my gosh, what will people think? My new neighbors? All of our friends? *I instantly felt shameful about this. I felt guilty and overwhelmed by everything. Matthew was loved by many. What will his patients do without him? He loved his patients.*

I never got him to get into the car. I've never felt such exhaustion in my life. I'm floating, I feel like I am watching a made-for-TV horror movie, and I don't like this movie. Turn it off. My life is over, I can't believe my powerful, strong, handsome, life-loving husband is really gone.

The kids said Matthew came in their rooms. It was early, must have been five a.m., I'm guessing. He gave them hugs goodbye. Grady's door was locked, so he didn't get a hug. Grady thinks if his door was unlocked, he would have had the wherewithal to save his dad again, like he did the night before. I don't think this. I think God was protecting Grady.

I had left a note on the kitchen counter. It said: Kids, I'm taking Dad to the hospital, be back soon. XO, Mom

I guess I called people to tell them the news; however, I don't remember doing this. Annie said my voice was high-pitched and that I didn't sound like myself. I was surprised when I got a text from a friend that I hadn't spoken to in years. The kids — they had posted on social media. "RIP Dad." Omigosh, I was not prepared for this.

Around 10:30 a.m. I decided to take a shower. Kids knocked on the bathroom door. I answered the door wrapped in a towel. All three of them were standing there. Grady said, "Mom, I got accepted to the University of Wyoming!" I was stunned. What a blessing but this was mystifying. Matthew would have been proud and happy for Grady. Thank you, God, for at least answering one of my prayers. This is bizarre.

- *University of Wyoming. Grady got his acceptance letter today*
- *Bright yellow sun that warms my heart and soul*
- *People in our house*

We made the Thanksgiving turkey. Why? This was so surreal. I know that we are all in shock. I feel as though I am having an out-of-body experience. It's like I am watching someone else's life on a TV show. I hate it. My younger brother Bo surprised me when he walked through the door that evening at seven. I gave him the biggest hug ever. We then sat in silence, staring at the walls. Nobody has words. I wonder: How did Bo get here all the way from Minnesota?

I somehow can feel God with me. I feel as though I am the lead character in a movie right now, and He is the producer, and I have to follow Him—I need to listen to Him. I have learned much about God during this crash course I've taken since arriving in North Carolina. God is love, and I can feel His love even though I feel gutted and broken.

It is 6 a.m. on November 29, the day after Thanksgiving. I am going to the gym. What else should I be doing? Is it bewildering that I'm going to go work out? Yes. I know it is. As I drive down the dark streets, starlight twinkling on this beautiful lake, the verse that is on repeat in my head is Thessalonians 16: "Rejoice always, 17: Pray without ceasing, 18: Give thanks in all circumstances; for this is the will of God in Christ Jesus."

My Jesus music is playing on the radio. I don't know how to do this, Lord. How can I thank you for this? I can't, but I can thank you for my children. Matthew had a gun or possibly even several of them—maybe he planted them outside earlier? I am not sure how this happened because I thought Bruce and Chris took all of the guns out of our house on Monday evening. He must have been planning this and hid a gun in the backyard. This is my theory. I am just so grateful that my kids did not get injured, they are all safe and sound asleep right now in their beds. My brother Bo is here. I am grateful for that, Lord. Help me. Please help me, and watch over me and the kids.

I guess my Edina High School best girlfriends are on the way here. I looked out the window of my home office, and I saw Debbie, who just arrived from Chicago. I ran out to greet her as her Uber pulled away. Dropping her bags, we hugged forever. We went on a walk. We were walking, talking, and I was telling her everything. Annie, Katie, Megan, and Beth arrived later on. Hugs, tears, food, wine. The house, this empty house, has been sad for so long. Now the house was filled with many tears. Only they were not just mine anymore.

I'm lucky to have such good girlfriends. They took me to Nordstrom to shop for a dress. I couldn't believe I was buying a dress for Matthew Gall's funeral. This can't be real. I was exhausted, and I thought to myself, being a doctor killed Matthew. He had at least nine concussions over his lifetime—and I never recognized the fact that he may have had mental illness possibly stemming from this. Depression was not Matthew's thing; I hardly ever saw Matthew sad. This is crazy, and I can't believe this is now my life.

A former neighbor texted me. It was a very upsetting text. She said something like: "Dearest Betsy, I have little details of what happened, but I am shattered for you and your children. I lived my childhood into my thirties with a father who threatened suicide if my mom ever left him. He also threatened to kill the six of us children as he believed he had nothing else to live for. My mom stayed with him to prevent this from happening. The rest of us were scarred for life. You live in fear every day of your life. No one knows what goes on behind closed doors. Take care of yourself. Take care of your children. Don't look back. If there is anything I can do to help, please let me know. My heart aches for you all."

OMG, seriously?! What the heck? People think we were living a double life? There were no marital issues, Matt and I were generally very happy people, yes, we moved for Matthew to make more money, for a fresh start, yes this is true—but we were not having financial trouble. Matthew was a cheery, happy-go-lucky guy who never threatened suicide or threatened to kill our kids. I was so unnerved by this message that I was shaking. I can't believe this. I felt embarrassed and shameful. I wanted to vomit. I was also furious. How dare she say, "Don't look back." I can't believe my husband is gone.

My reply was: "I am sorry to hear about your childhood. How awful! That was NOT the case with Matthew at all. Matthew was the most loving, caring, kind husband and father. We came to North Carolina full of hope for a new job and new adventure. I think Matthew felt trapped and he couldn't sleep. He was so smart, but he couldn't turn his brain off. He quickly fell into a deep, dark depression, which was unexpected and so not him."

The neighbor replied something along the lines of: "It's hard to believe that it can happen this quickly. I think of him first thing when I wake up. Very few people could do what Matt did. I don't call it a job because I doubt that is the way he saw it. I know he was very compassionate toward his patients. He seems to have an almost exuberance or passion for the things he loved, like his music. It makes it hard to picture him in such a dark place with no hope. We are all complex human beings. I hope he has found peace, and hope that you and the children will in time find peace, too."

I guess her last message redeemed her; she is a really nice person. But I was very hurt. Ugh, can't believe I have to deal with all of this speculation on top of missing my sweet Matthew.

My kids. All I can think about is how this will affect my kids. I don't know anyone who has ever died by suicide. I don't understand it.

I learned later that there are 30,000 gun-related deaths per year, The breakdown of those deaths gives us perspective—when compared to other causes of death:

- In 2020 alone, more than 45,000 Americans died by gunshot, whether by homicide or suicide, more than any other year on record. This represents a 25% increase from five years prior, and a 40-plus increase from 2010. [1]
- Of the total, about 54 percent were suicides.[2]

---

[1] https://www.bbc.com/news/world-us-canada-41488081

[2] https://health.ucdavis.edu/what-you-can-do/facts.html

Chapter 8
Excellent Article about Doctor Suicide

Our friend from the lake found an article that is being texted around our friend group. Its title is: "Why '*Happy*' Doctors Die by Suicide," written by Pamela Wible, MD. It is about a "masterful" surgeon, Dr. Benjamin Shaffer, who "had it all." *We had it all*, I think to myself. **Why "Happy" Doctors Die by Suicide**, Written by Dr. Pamela Wible, MD – used with permission.

He was the go-to sports guy in Washington, DC. A masterful surgeon with countless academic publications, he trained orthopedic surgeons across the world, and was the top physician for professional sports teams and Olympians.

Dr. Benjamin Shaffer had it all.

Yet Ben was more than a stellar surgeon. He was a kind, sweet, brilliant, and sensitive soul who could relate to anyone—from inner city children to Supreme Court justices. He was gorgeous and magnetic with a sense of humor and a zest for life that was contagious. Most of all, he loved helping people. Patients came to him in pain and left his office laughing. They called him "Dr. Smiles."

Ben was at the top of his game when he ended his life. So why did he die?

Underneath his irresistible smile, Ben hid a lifetime of anxiety amid his professional achievements. He had recently been weaned off anxiolytics and was suffering from rebound anxiety and insomnia—sleeping just a few hours per night, and trying to operate and treat patients each day. Then his psychiatrist retired and passed him on to a new one.

Eight days before he died, his psychiatrist prescribed two new drugs that worsened his insomnia, increased his anxiety, and led to paranoia. He was told he would need medication for the rest of his life. Devastated, Ben feared he would never have a normal life. He told his sister it was "game over."

Ben admitted he was suicidal with a plan, though he told his psychiatrist he wouldn't act on it. Ben knew he should check himself into a hospital, but was panicked. He was terrified he would lose his patients, his practice, his marriage, and that everyone in DC—team owners, players, patients, colleagues—would find out about his mental illness, and he would be shunned.

The night before he died, Ben requested the remainder of the week off to rest. His colleagues were supportive, yet he was ashamed. He slept that night, but awoke wiped out on May 20, 2015. After driving his son to school, he came home and hanged himself on a bookcase. He left no note. He left behind his wife and two children.

I feel a kinship with Ben, partly because I used to suffer from chronic anxiety that I hid under academic achievements, but mostly because I'm a cheerful doctor who was once a suicidal physician too. In 2004 I thought I was the only suicidal physician in the world—until 2012 when I found myself at the memorial for our third doctor suicide in my small town. Despite his very public death, nobody uttered the word suicide aloud. Yet everyone kept whispering "Why?" I wanted to know why. So I started counting doctor suicides. Within a few minutes I counted 10. Five years later I had a list of 547. By January this year, I had 757 cases on my registry. As of today, that number is 1,013.

(Keynote delivered at Chicago Orthopedic Symposium reviews data and simple solutions to prevent doctor suicides.)

High doctor suicide rates have been reported since 1858.[3] Yet 160 years later the root causes of these suicides remain unaddressed. Physician suicide is a global public health crisis. More than one million Americans lose their

---

[3] Bucknill, J.C. and Tuke, D.H. 1858. *A Manual of Psychological Medicine*.

doctors each year to suicide—just in the U.S.[4] Many doctors have lost several colleagues to suicide. One doctor told me he lost eight physicians during his career, with no chance to grieve.

Of these 1,013 suicides, 888 are physicians and 125 are medical students. The majority (867) are in the USA and 146 are international. Surgeons have the greatest number of suicides on my registry; then anesthesiologists. [5]

However, when accounting for numbers of active physicians per specialty, anesthesiologists are more than twice as likely to die by suicide than any other physician. Surgeons are number two, then emergency medicine physicians, obstetrician/gynecologists, and psychiatrists. [6]

For every woman who dies by suicide on my registry, we lose four men. Suicide methods vary by specialty, region, and gender. Women prefer overdose. In the USA, men use firearms. Jumping is popular in New York City. In India, doctors are found hanging from ceiling fans. Male anesthesiologists are at highest risk among all physicians. Most anesthesiologists overdose. Many are found dead inside hospital call rooms.

[4] Wible, P., 2014. "When doctors commit suicide, it's often hushed up." *Washington Post.*

[5] Wible, P. Keynote, 19th Annual Chicago Orthopedic Symposium, 8/18/18

[6] AAMC Physician Specialty Data Report. 2016.

Doctor suicides on the registry were submitted to me during a six-year period (2012–2018) by families, friends, and colleagues who knew the deceased. After speaking to thousands of suicidal physicians since 2012 on my informal doctor suicide hotline, and analyzing registry data, I discovered surprising themes—many unique to physicians.

Public perception maintains that doctors are successful, intelligent, wealthy, and immune from the problems of the masses. To patients, it is inconceivable that doctors would have the highest suicide rate of any profession.[7]

Even more baffling, "happy" doctors are dying by suicide. Many doctors who kill themselves appear to be the most optimistic, upbeat, and confident people. Just back from Disneyland, just bought tickets for a family cruise, just gave a thumbs up to the team after a successful surgery—and hours later they shoot themselves in the head.

Doctors are masters of disguise and compartmentalization.

Turns out some of the happiest people—especially those who spend their days making other people happy—may be masking their own despair. Reading this excerpt from the 1858 Manual of Psychological Medicine, I'm reminded of so many brilliant doctors I've lost to suicide: [1]

[7] American Psychiatric Association (APA) 2018. Abstract 1-227, presented May 5, 2018.

"Carlini, a French actor of reputation, consulted a physician to whom he was unknown, on account of the attacks of profound melancholy to which he was subject. The doctor, among other things, recommended the diversion of the Italian comedy; 'for,' said he, 'your distemper must be rooted indeed, if the acting of the lively Carlini does not remove it.' 'Alas!' ejaculated the miserable patient, 'I am the very Carlini whom you recommend me to see; and, while I am capable of filling Paris with mirth and laughter, I am myself the dejected victim of melancholy and chagrin.'"

Many of our most inspiring and visionary leaders—artists, actors, even doctors—suffer from mental illness.

Yet students enter medical school with their mental health on par with or better than their peers. Suicide is an occupational hazard in medicine. Doctors develop on-the-job PTSD—especially in emergency medicine. Patient deaths—even with no medical error—may lead to self-loathing. Suicide is the ultimate self-punishment. Humans make mistakes. When doctors make mistakes, they are publicly shamed in court, on television, and in newspapers (that live online forever). As doctors, we suffer the agony of harming someone else—unintentionally—for the rest of our lives

Blaming doctors increases suicides. Words like "burnout" and "resilience" are employed by medical institutions to blame and shame doctors while deflecting their own accountability for inhumane working conditions in failing health systems. When doctors are punished for occupationally induced mental health wounds, they become even more desperate.

If physicians do seek help, they risk being disciplined. Doctors rightfully fear lack of confidentiality when receiving mental health care as private conversations with therapists could be turned over to medical boards and illegally accessed by their supervisors via electronic medical records at their institutions. So physicians drive out of town, pay cash, and use fake names in paper charts to hide from state boards, hospitals, and insurance plans that interrogate doctors about their mental health and may prevent or delay state licensure, hospital privileges, and health plan participation.

With a great work ethic until their last breath, doctors are often checking in on patients, reviewing test results, and dictating charts minutes before orchestrating their own suicides. Many leave apologetic heartfelt letters detailing the reasons for their suicide for friends, family, and staff. One orthopedic surgeon simply wrote: "I'm sorry I couldn't fix everyone."

Doctors choose suicide to end their pain (not because they want to die). Suicide is preventable if we stop the secrecy, stigma, and punishment. In absence of support, doctors make impulsive decisions to end their pain permanently. I asked several male physicians who survived their suicides, "How long after you decided to kill yourself did you take action—overdose on pills or pull the trigger?" The answer: 3 to 5 minutes.

Ignoring doctor suicides leads to more doctor suicides. Let's not wait until the last few minutes of a doctor's life when heroic interventions are required. Most physician suicides are multifactorial involving a cascade of events that unfold months to years prior. So reach out to "happy" doctors today—especially male anesthesiologists and surgeons who are least likely to cry or ask for help.

Chapter 9
The Kids Are Scared and Ask Questions

November 30, 2019—Gavin, my son who turned 15 two weeks ago, stops me on the stairs. *"Mom, what's going to happen to us?"* I hug him, *"Oh sweetheart, it's going to be okay. I promise you."*

"No," he says, *"I mean how are we going to live? You don't have a job. Grandpa told me that we will have to tighten our belts and that I'll have to get a job."*

Oh, for the love of God. I tell Gavin not to listen to Grandpa, but for the first time, I wonder and think, What is going to happen to us? *He's right, I don't have a job.*

The next morning, I'm standing in my kitchen with my brother. I tell him about the conversation with Gavin. Bo says, *"Well, you had life insurance, didn't you?"* *"Yes,"* I say, but I don't think it will pay out because Matt killed himself. Bo thinks that's not true—and thankfully, Bo was right. We drop Sophie off at a birthday party. I can't believe we are going about our *normal life—but what are we supposed to do? Sit at home and stare at the walls? No, we must keep going.*

Today I have the dismal job of writing Matt's obituary. He was 49. Feeling overwhelmed, I have to ask for help. We have a talented friend who is in PR; she can help. I've asked for input from everyone in the family. After many edits it reads:

Gall, Matthew Taylor, M.D. 49, devoted husband, father, son, brother, colleague, "fun guy," and dear friend, died on November 28, 2019. Matthew was born on July 9, 1970, in Beaver Dam, WI, to parents Bruce and Elaine Gall. He is survived by his loving wife of 20 years, Betsy Gall, his wonderful children Grady, Gavin and Sophie, his parents Bruce and Elaine Gall, his brother Christian (Diane) and Andrew Gall, his in-laws Michael and Gail Lewis, Ryan (Kristin), Caden and Greyson Lewis, Bo (Melissa) Emmy Lou and TJ Lewis, and an abundance of friends and patients. Matthew was a successful and caring physician for 16 years. He dedicated his life to his patients and treating their cancer. He felt honored to help those in need. He loved each and every one of his patients. Matthew possessed a remarkable joie de vivre, the joy for life. He was a considerate man who loved his family deeply and was a fiercely loyal friend to many. He loved celebrating holidays with his family and enjoyed live music. He loved God. He was a patriot who deeply loved America. He had an unbridled enthusiasm for his Pittsburgh Steelers and Wisconsin Badgers. He loved playing rugby, perfecting his grilling skills, mountain biking, spending time at his beloved cabin and traveling the world while always managing to maintain the perfect lawn. Matthew had a knack for setting the perfect mood with music. He was happiest when he was spending time with friends, family, and his dog, Liberty. He made every room brighter with his spirit and joie de vivre, joy for life, and will be forever missed. A celebration service will be held for Matthew on Thursday, December 12 at Colonial Church of Edina, 6200 Colonial Way, Edina MN at 11:30 a.m. Memorials preferred to Angel Foundation, UW Men's Rugby Club or Lone Survivor Organization.

Bruce and Elaine aren't thrilled with the picture I chose. But I can't look through all of these pictures—it's way too hard. This picture was taken at our old private school fundraising gala; he was happy that night and happy to be there. I don't think Bruce likes the bow tie. Matt didn't wear a lot of bow ties, but he sure did like to dress up.

Looking back on the obituary, I missed many of Matthew's accomplishments. He was a graduate of UW Madison with degrees in biochemistry and molecular biology. He graduated from the Medical College of Wisconsin with a doctorate in medicine, an internship and residency at University of Illinois at Chicago. He was a graduate of the University of Minnesota with a master's degree in clinical research. He was a member of many societies and associations. I even forgot to mention all of his accomplishments at The Group. He dedicated his entire professional life to his patients, who he loved dearly. He was compassionate. The only thing I can think of is all of that knowledge in his brain—it is gone. Vanished off the face of the earth with one single gunshot. All of his oncology patients are left without their beloved doctor. My kids have no father. My husband is dead. Matt dedicated his entire life to saving lives by being an oncology physician. This is not right, not right at all.

The days and months after Matthew died seem like a blur. Looking back, I am not sure how I did it. I prayed. Every morning when I opened my eyes, I thanked God. Hard some days to be thankful in the midst of all my pain and sorrow—but there is always something to be grateful for. "One foot in front of the other" became my motto.

On December 5, I get up and work out, Sophie is staying home from school to work on her eulogy, and I am walking Liberty at 6 a.m. while talking to my Mom on my cell phone. I'm really glad that I was talking to people in Minnesota about Matthew. I couldn't talk to my friends here; it was a secret that Matthew was sick. How would I have explained to people that my oncologist husband was sick with depression, of all things? We moved here for him to help build a practice. I've requested a luncheon with my seven new North Carolina girlfriends. We are going to Missy's. I'm tired, I talk and pray in the car a lot. So many texts and emails and Facebook notes to keep up with. I'm literally exhausted. My life is going to be very bland without Matthew. It's going to be very quiet without him. All of our dreams, shattered.

Missy's luncheon was amazing and healing for me because I know these girls have my back. Missy, Cynda, Jennifer, Lisa, Dawn, Angela, and Shelly were all there. I told them everything from the beginning. How we left Minnesota for a fresh start in a warmer climate. I read Matt's obituary to them and explained that six months ago we were like them, living perfectly normal lives. I thanked them. I love these girls. I told them that I didn't know how I would need them, but I would need them because now I was a single mom. That is freaking crazy to think about. Divine intervention was for sure at the center of all of us meeting each other.

After lunch, I picked up the death certificates, ugh. More flowers were delivered. We went out to dinner with some other Minnesota girlfriends that were kind enough to fly in and help; however, I can't help but think soon all of these people will be gone. Then I'll have to stare at death right out my back door.

On the way to school the next day, Gavin asked, "Mom, who is going to help me tie my tie?" Oh man, this is tough. All I can think about is my kids. How will this trauma affect them? This is a life-altering situation that has changed all of us for-ever—and it sucks.

Poor Matthew, he must have felt trapped. This entire ordeal has been the perfect storm. I feel guilty—because I was the one to find the recruiter that led us to this chapter in our lives.

I talked to my Minnesota friend Kelly for an hour and a half. She is a grief counselor and knew Matthew well. She is a friend of The Group there, and I've volunteered with Kelly at Angel Foundation for years. Angel Foundation helps Minnesota cancer patients with nonmedical needs. Kelly told me that Matthew saved lives while here on earth, and he will continue to do so even now that he's gone. I believe that, too. Something good will eventually come out of this horrific event. Someday.

I have to work on the program for the funeral. I can't keep up with all the texts, Facebook messages, emails, and phone calls. People are devastated. Everyone is shocked and sad—but no one more than me. Matt was my best friend. My life will now be bland and colorless. How could he leave me like this? Not sure I'll ever, ever understand.

I guess I have to go to the social security office? My kids will get social security. I had no idea this was available to me. Thank God that my girlfriends set up the appointment for me. I need health insurance, too. The girls explain to me that I'll need to tap into the Affordable Care Act. Matthew really didn't think this through. He wasn't thinking; he would be mortified knowing I had to do all of this shit. I'm having a hard time, feeling like I'm in a movie watching somebody else's life. It's an awful, awful movie. This can't be my life.

I took Gavin to the mall, made returns, had a phone call with my sister-in-law Silla. I'm crying in the car. I cried as I walked through the mall, too. My tears don't seem to stop. Tears are liquid love, and they don't stop streaming down my face. Grady called me, telling me that Matthew didn't use his (Grady's) gun. Grady was relieved that his dad didn't use his gun to shoot himself. I had no idea he was worried about this. This really freaks me out, all three kids will have different issues to deal with. Oh my goodness, this is what trauma looks like up close.

Diane and I had wine last night. Diane had notes on obsessive compulsive disorder that perfectly described Matthew Gall to a "T." How did I never notice this before? I received a nice note from a partner of Matthew's at The Group in Minnesota. I have flashbacks of Matthew in the backyard. We have lots of flowers and cookie baskets, as this stuff keeps coming. I'm happy that The Group sent this email to their employees. It reads:

From: The Group
Sent: Saturday, December 7, 2019
Subject: Death of Former Staff Physician

We are saddened to learn of the reported suicide of Matthew Gall, MD. The tragic and sudden circumstances of Dr. Gall's death may cause a range of reactions among our workplace, so with the family's permission we are sharing the facts as we know them and are offering support for those who might need it. Dr. Gall had worked for this group for sixteen years. On Thursday, November 28th, he died. We may never know all the factors leading to this tragedy; however, experts agree that in nearly all suicides there is no single cause or simple explanation.

Dr. Gall's memorial service will be held on Thursday, December 12. Dr. Gall's family shared with us his obituary to pass along to all staff and providers. The family would like to welcome all of his friends and colleagues who wish to share in the celebration of his life.

Some of you may be having difficulty coping with the sudden loss of one of our workplace family. Some of you may have experienced this sort of tragedy or suffering in your personal lives. Our Employee Assistance Program is available to assist with support to each of you at this time. Counselors are available to support us and answer any questions you may have. For those who would like to talk about what has happened, our HR team is available to you.

This was signed by the President, Medical Director, and HR Director

Sunday, Dec. 8, 2019. I can't sleep, I'm up at two a.m. thinking about this note that was sent. Doctors are not easily replaced, and if doctors are killing themselves at alarming rates, what are we going to do? American desperately needs more physicians. I feel like this is an epidemic that nobody is talking about. I read the Star Tribune *newspaper obituary comments on my iPad while I'm in bed. Sophie sleeps with me. I love hearing her gentle snoring. Liberty has been dreaming lots, too. She also sleeps with me, and this is a first. I never even let Liberty upstairs, for fear of getting dog hair all over—and now she is in my bed. Things that used to matter to me don't matter anymore. Everything has been put into perspective.*

Chapter 10
Going through the Motions

I'm curious as to what a nurse who had worked with Matthew recently will say. She said she had prayed about whether to contact me, and God told her to reach out. She called me the other day. I'm here in the Bible Belt. God is all around me. I think many people are upset with Matthew. I'm not—he wasn't himself…he was literally tormented. I only wish we'd left North Carolina sooner—it was "a swing and a miss," as our lawyer friend stated. Why couldn't Matthew see this? We could have gone to the lake, but he kept pushing, pushing, pushing for us and for his patients. Oh Matt, I'm so sorry. I'm going to church. More later.

Church service was beautiful. Ask, pray, peace, these are the words floating through my mind today. Cynda and Auntie Di came over to talk about Liberty. Cynda will take care of her while we go back to Minnesota for the funeral. What am I going to do with this house? That backyard, I want the trees and that gross hot tub to be gone. I was tired all day. I found letters that I wrote to Matt in 2006 and 2016 explaining what to do if I died. He'd be lost if I died first. He didn't know how to pay bills, he was never concerned about the minutia, he didn't even know our passwords. We used to joke about how he didn't know how to use the ATM. Matthew and I had set up revocable living trusts together, but he had handled the life insurance. This is astounding, he made sure we'd be taken care of.

Friends are talking about Matt's concussions and the odd things he'd sometimes say. He could at times be emotional. At the end of his life, I wasn't sure what was real and what wasn't. Spoke to Matthew's Mom Elaine today. I feel bad for her and Bruce. Matt was their shining star. It is Christmas time and people are dropping everything for me, and I can't believe it.

I feel rested; I got six hours of sleep. Off to the gym. I talk to God on my way to my workout in the dark. I listen to worship music all the time. Packing, shipping skis, the list of to-do items is long. I know that eventually I'm going to be okay. Forgot to mention Grady's appointment with his therapist yesterday. She works with kids and has a little cabin or "office" in the woods. I feel as though it is a spiritual place. She is sweet and intuitive. He didn't say if he liked her or not, but he's smoking pot again — I'm not happy, but I'm managing my feelings.

At home I'm simply going through the motions. Laundry, nail appointment, dishes, dog walking — crossing things off my list. Had an afternoon call with my Mom and the Minnesota pastor who will conduct Matthew's service about planning the funeral. Tears flow nonstop. Feelings of anguish and sadness *permeate within my bones. Gavin is off to a Young Life meeting, Grady is high, and Soph went to the basketball game. Kids are still in shock. Gavin looks at pictures all the time. I can't bear to look at any. Sophie is excited to be going back home. Grady sits and plays video games. This is painful.*

Auntie Di slept over last night, and I had only one glass of wine. Bedtime is 9:15. I woke during the night thinking of Matt and the actual shooting. This haunts me. It's like I am watching it in slow motion, even though I didn't see Matthew pull the trigger. I didn't find or even see his body. I'm constantly going over the events in my mind. Over and over again. Up at 3:45 a.m. doing my morning spiritual readings, drinking copious amounts of coffee, journaling, prayer, gym, and packing, as our flight leaves at 4:45 this afternoon. We are finally going home today. This is unreal that on December 10th we are flying to Minneapolis for my husband's funeral. It's Christmas time.

I spoke to the kids during the drive to school. It hit me that they'd never been to a funeral—and now they are going to their dad's. I explained how funerals work and what to expect. I told them that they will be the "stars" of the show and will have a ton of attention on them. I told them that this is only a moment in time, and that time heals, and that they will go on to live beautiful, full, happy lives. I told them that we can't define Dad by how he died; we need to remember how he lived.

I referred to Scot's death back in 1992. Scot was my on-again, off-again high school and college boyfriend of five years. It was his death in a car accident 27 years prior that gave me insight on what to expect of the grief process. If you had told me then that I'd be married, with three beautiful children and the cutest dog in the world after he died, I wouldn't have ever believed it. But time does heal. And we need to put one foot in front of the other, as hard as it may be.

Sophie had tears. She hates being sad, so she masks it. I have to watch her closely. I also told the kids that they are still in shock—and the hard work will come later when everyone goes back to their normal lives. I think to myself: and my children will have to adjust to a new normal, and it will not be easy. I'm the luckiest Mom in the world to have them as my children, I love them more than anything.

Back home, cleaning, laundry, dropping off Liberty at Cynda's, packing, and organizing take up my time. I received the life insurance packet in the mail—it is all so unbelievable. Money to live, but my partner who I dreamed of building a life with here in North Carolina is gone. What is home going to be like now? The insurance money, I am so grateful for it but it feels strange, this is not a fun way to get money.

Heading home for the funeral, I am so sad at the airport because when we first arrived here at this exact airport only four months ago, we were full of hope for a brighter future. I'm super crabby. I snapped at Gavin. Kids are really excited to go home. Diane often tells the kids, "Make good choices." I love that woman. She's been amazing for me. I pray that my kids will make good choices, as I know that they will face many challenges moving forward. I told the kids about Dad and how he always made the sign of the cross while boarding the airplane. They all did it.

It's raining in here—but -9 °F at home.

We look at old videos of Dad, Sophie has saved his voicemails. I looked through our last few weeks of texts. He knew he was losing it. I did too—but at the same time I really didn't because this was Matt Gall after all. We had a plan, but he couldn't hang on. I emailed my pastor's assistant earlier. I found Matt's grandfather's Bible that he gave Matt at his medical college graduation. It sat on his bedside table with an inscription that I want the pastor to read at the funeral.

We are all going to die, we are all essentially terminal. But 49 years old? That's too young. Who am I going to talk with about our kids with, and all of our dreams?

- ◎ *The in-law's big Cadillac because it holds all of us and our luggage*
- ◎ *Uninterrupted time with my kids held captive in the car while we drive*
- ◎ *Darling neighbor to take in the mail*
- ◎ *Cynda for sending cute videos of Liberty*
- ◎ *Warm coats*
- ◎ *Looking at my kids' faces, who are ecstatic to see their friends*
- ◎ *This journal*
- ◎ *Vision and intuition*

Today is December 12, 2019 — and we're going to Matthew Gall's funeral. How can this be? I've got to get through this day. I did sleep for six hours, thanks to sleep medication, which is the only way I can fall asleep. I have to be strong, faithful, and lean on God, then tomorrow I can start to put my shattered life and my shattered heart back together. I'll put away my shattered dreams and move forward, alone.

Yesterday, out doing errands with the boys, I came within one inch of crashing that stupid rental car. Lord, I know you are up there guiding and protecting me every inch of the way. Matthew will continue to watch over me, and God will continue to guide me. Please Lord, help me navigate this life and help my children reach their dreams. They are my everything, and I am extremely proud of them. I can't believe I'm going to Matt Gall's funeral today. My Matthew. How can this be? You left a huge gaping hole in our lives. I simply can't comprehend that I am going to your funeral. It's snowing outside, and I must admit, it's quite pretty.

This morning I am going to the gym and getting Starbucks afterward, and I'll leave the barista money to pay it forward. Home to Mom and Dad's, kids are getting ready. Ryan, my brother, picks us up, and we tell funny stories about Dad on the way to the church. In the hearth room, it's family only — and my entire extended family is there. Galls, the Lewis family, Auntie Kiki, Auntie Sally, Uncle Tom, Pat, and all of my cousins and other relatives. It was good to see them. My family is together again. Matt did that. Recently we have not been in the best place as a family, but now we are together again as a family. Matthew would have liked that.

I'm struggling with Matt's last few days. I was extremely tired. He had freaked me out so many times but I didn't think he'd actually kill himself…but I felt something bad was going to happen. His health care directive states: As long as my mind works, and I can be a physician, keep me alive. Then I reread the letters I wrote to him in 2006 and 2016. They say that if Matt's reading them, something bad has happened to me. At the end, Matt didn't think he could be a doctor anymore. And that was who he was at the core.

Matt's mind was gone at the end. It was almost as if he was in a psychosis state. I told people that Matt never did anything half-way—so of course the depression that hit him was fast, hard, furious, and dark. I'm happy and relieved that his parents got to see him before he died. I wish we'd never come to North Carolina; I wish we'd done things differently. Everything changed on Thanksgiving Day, and my life and the kids' lives will never be the same.

The funeral was simply beautiful. Grace. Breathe. Pray. Breathe. Pray. Give us Peace. Grace. These are the words I kept repeating to myself over and over again in my mind to keep me from becoming hysterical.

Our pastor did a beautiful job. The fact that we discussed depression was difficult, but the right thing to do. There must have been 800–1,000 people at the service. I think it was standing-room only. Matt had five good guy friends, and each one spoke at the service and did an amazing job. But the kids, oh our three kids, were the best with their eulogies. I sat there, my heart was bursting with pride, how brave the three of them were. The flowers and the music was all simply beautiful.

The pastor said, "On the day Matt graduated from medical school in Wisconsin, his Grandfather McLaughlin, who was a pastor, gave him a Bible. The scriptures we have heard today tell us that God will be with us in all circumstances. It's God's plan to be with us. It's God's promise."

Then the pastor read his grandfather's inscription: "Dear Matthew, You have received much education out of books throughout these past years in medical school. I am giving you this book of life's wisdom, and you'll get education on how to live your life, as God is the creator of all wisdom."

The pastor continued: "Matthew always had encouraging words for everybody. So keep telling Matthew's stories because he is still here with us."

♦   ♦   ♦

I think about how Matthew frequently talked about wanting to live to be 100 years old like his grandfather did. So it's incredibly ironic that he took his own life. Especially since he dedicated his entire life as an oncologist to preserving and saving lives. This makes absolutely no sense to me. I can't seem to wrap my head around it.

Off to the local country club for the reception. The sheer volume of people there was overwhelming. People stood and waited to get a word with me. I was honored. I was overcome with love and prayers as I held onto my grandmother Binna's rosary that my aunt Sally gave to me.

- *My iPad*
- *Minnesota: I'm grateful for Minnesota even if it is -9°F*
- *Tears from friends who love you so*
- *The softly fallen snow*
- *Pretty music*
- *Beautiful friends*
- *Beautiful friends*
- *Beautiful friends*
- *Amazing Grace*
- *Wonderful stories about my husband*
- *Laughter*
- *Memories of a beautiful life*
- *Be still and know that I am God*
- *Old friends*
- *New friends*
- *Family, all of them*

To the doctor with the golden stethoscope…I could not find a
single picture without you smiling in it.
This is how I will always remember you.
Always and forever, B.

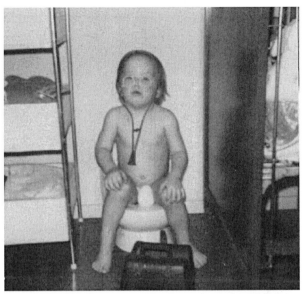

Toddler Matt as a young wanna be doctor

Matthew's 11th Birthday

The Ultimate Badger Warrior and roommate Jon

College Rugby UW Madison

Medical College of Wisconsin Graduation with parents

Matthew as a resident

Wedding Day; Minnesota Bride Magazine
Elizabeth Grubb Photography

Matthew with brother Chris and parents Bruce & Elaine

Betsy and Matthew the early years

Grady's favorite photo of him and his dad

Gavin's favorite photo of him and his dad

Sophie's favorite photo of her and her dad

Ski trip Big Sky Montana

Nephew Andrew, Brother Chris and Matthew
at our lake house

Lewis Family Christmas

Betsy and Auntie Di

Matthew at Steelers Super Bowl

Dr. Foley & Matthew Road Trip

Matthew's Partners at The Group

At Matthew's Happy Place aka the Lake House

Last photo with Chris & Di North Carolina

Minnesota girls in Grand Cayman Beth, Megan, Debbie,
Ann, Katie & Betsy

North Carolina girls Jennifer, Lisa, Betsy, Angie, Cynda, Dawn & Shelly

First North Carolina Friend Missy

The Illusion of the Perfect Profession ◆ 147

College Bestie Sarah

Matthew Grilling at Lake House in Northern Minnesota

Last Family Vacation Jamaica

Obituary photo 2019

Missing Matthew Forever Grady, Gavin, Sophie, Liberty
& Betsy, photo by Dietrich Gesk

Chapter 11
Another First: Christmas

December 25, 2019. I'm awake again with a blank, thud sort of feeling in my heart. Merry Christmas. Debbie sent me a book. I didn't want to read it, but I did. I found it very helpful. It was called Life after Suicide, *by Dr. Jennifer Ashton. It's about Dr. Ashton, "Good Morning America" Chief Medical correspondent's journey through her ex-husband, Dr. Rob Ashton's suicide. Rob was a brilliant thoracic and cardiac surgeon who also died by suicide, jumping from the George Washington bridge on February 11, 2017. In her book, Jennifer talks about others left behind by suicide.*

As hard as the book was to read, it gave me hope. I need hope right now. It's all I have to hang on to.

What a joke…Merry Christmas. I'm NOT feeling it. I badly want to fast forward now and know that my kids will be okay. I'm going to church; maybe that will make me feel better. I have to give these Christmas presents to my family—but it's hard to do without having any joy in your heart. Maybe if I keep watching the cute videos of years past, I can smile. I came home from church and gave the entire family some special presents from me and Matt. My kids are excited about the trip to Maui for spring break. My parents' house is always decorated so perfectly for Christmas. It's warm and cozy yet colorless, quiet, and blah without Matthew here. He loved the holidays and always wore his plaid Christmas pants and a red sweater. The holidays…they will never be the same.

December 28, 2019. Roads are awful, but I still went to the gym. I read all of my texts with Matt from the week before he died. I had tried to encourage him. This whole thing is so messed up. Should the hospital be held responsible for letting him leave? He was suicidal, was in the emergency room only hours before he took his own life, and of course, he lied to the ER doctor—he knew what the consequences would be if he didn't. Matthew served the medical community for over twenty years, and I feel as though the medical community failed him. I had even left a message with Dr. Foley in Minnesota asking him to call the emergency room in North Carolina that evening. I told him he needed to call the on-call doctor and explain how sick Matthew was. Dr. Foley didn't get my message until it was too late. This was the perfect storm.

After my workout, I met Dr. Mrachek, the anesthesiologist with whom I had connected with on Facebook, a mere nine days before Matthew died. He gives speeches on physician suicide. We met at the coffee shop during the awful ice/rainstorm. I wasn't going to let the bad weather stop me from meeting this guy.

When I saw him, I grabbed and hugged him, which was weird because I'd never met him before. He's handsome and articulate. He feels as though it's his mission to help spread the word about physician suicide. I'm tired. Waves of grief roll over me. I'm not the same person I was—and I never will be. I told him everything. He listened with care and understood everything I said. It felt good to talk to someone who "gets it."

I went to a friend's birthday party, and I tried to have fun but couldn't. Old neighbors were there. Now I dislike some people that I actually used to really like—because they are so stupid. Funny how people treat you after a tragic event. Some people say the dumbest things. People are looking at me differently…I can feel it.

On December 31, 2020, Gavin and I drove up to the lake on the most gorgeous sunny day. Grady and Sophie had other plans and stayed home. I wasn't happy about that, but I don't have control over anything right now. Not a cloud in the sky and warm at 20 °F. I talked on the phone to Beth for an hour during the drive, and I am lucky to have her as a best friend. Gav listened to music. When we arrived at our lake house, a flood of emotions slammed me like a freight train. It was beautiful, but the "mancave" is packed with memories of Matthew. We last left the lake on July 31st, five months ago to the day, full of hopes and dreams for a brighter, easier life. Memories flood my mind of Matt grilling at his favorite spot on earth, our walks and talks to the mailbox, our dreams about the future. How could he be so stupid to give that all up? Why did I help him find that awful job? I hate myself.

If only we'd stayed in Minnesota and stuck it out. I really am still shocked that Matthew took his own life, and doing so, he completely ruined many lives. I feel like I'll never be happy again. His photo albums from when he was a little boy were sitting on the table, which is odd. We found a letter from his grandfather written on the day Matthew was born. Waiting for us were the lawn signs I'd given him as "joke" presents. This place is all him: the motor bikes, the record player, his kegerator—Matt always had cold beer on tap, the Pittsburgh Steeler stuff was littered throughout. I feel like I'm going to die, I really do. This is hard, I feel as though I am suffocating. Tonight, we will be meeting friends for my first New Year's without my husband. Now many "firsts" are over: Thanksgiving, Christmas, and soon New Year's. I want to check them off the list. I guess I'm grateful for that.

After dinner we went to a friend's cabin and played a silly meme game. A friend of Matt's said the word suicide last night, in reference to the game. It felt uncomfortably odd, like an elephant in the room. Depression was another word. My heart sank. I'm exhausted, and now I'm getting a cold. I need sleep, but I can't sleep. I want him back. Not sure how I'm going to handle all of this stuff. Who will grill? Who will drive the boat? Who will take the kids tubing? I'm feeling overwhelmed and somber. I can only hope and pray that this next year will be better.

On January 6, 2020, we arrived back in North Carolina. Leaving Minnesota wasn't so hard, with the snow and the cloudiness. Saying goodbye to Mom and Dad wasn't the easiest, but getting out of living in their lower level felt good. Chris picked us up from the airport. All of us were excited to see our dog, Liberty. As we pulled up to our street, I burst into a thousand tears. Topiary trees, a wreath, my lawn looked perfect, pansies, and flower pots by my garage doors, flowers on my table in the backyard, and a gorgeous potted rose bush sat on the patio. My seven North Carolinian girlfriends had done this…to surprise me. "To let the happy in!" they said. I'm beyond blessed, and overcome with gratitude for these women. I feel the love. Chris and Di had lunch waiting for us—we loved up our dog who was trying to be mad at us for being gone for so long, but she was happy to see us, I know.

I thought coming back would be easy. It isn't. Soph and Gav left immediately for friends' houses to sleep over. Grady then asked if he could go to out to eat with friends—of course I said yes. Being home alone was a little scary. TVs don't work, and it's too quiet here. I heard a door shut upstairs, making me wonder, are there spirits in my house? I texted Grady: "I'm scared," and he came back early to be with me. I'm thankful for him. That kid can be such a love when he wants to be!

I sobbed all the way to church yesterday. I thought about how my life is now quiet, boring, and bland. I miss him. I wish we'd never left Minnesota. But Minnesota wasn't good for Grady, and he knows that. I looked through Matt's closet and smelled his clothes. Oh Lord, how am I supposed to do this? I have to raise these three kiddos on my own. Please help me.

I took Grady to his therapist's little cabin in the woods. I love this lady, yet I hardly even know her. Grady said she's "pretty cool." As I stood on her steps, and cried and I told her I wish I could hyper speed through this time—she reminded me that it's important to go through it. And then today my readings are such: He, the faithful God and me: "When you come to the waters you will not go down, but through…." I guess that is what I'm doing now.

Lots of calls and texts yesterday. I feel loved, but this is hard. I miss Matthew, and my life now—it's simply sad, and I still feel like I'm in a dream or some horror movie. Today I'm off to deal with the estate. I don't feel good. I know I need to sleep more. It's not hard to fall asleep, but hard to stay asleep. Kids are headed back to school today. Normalcy, a routine, happiness, these are all things I hope for. Dear God, please help me use my voice in the calm, correct way for my kids. Please help my kids Lord, please protect me and my family. Please God, help us!

Yesterday I went to the courthouse only to be told I didn't need to open the estate. They are so confused at the courthouse, telling me that there are complications because our revocable living trust was established in Minnesota, and now we are in North Carolina. Bureaucracy is a such a pain in the ass. They need a special department for widows only.

I went to the car dealership to have them fix the locks on my car and ended up buying a new-but-used car. My car hadn't *worked properly since arriving in North Carolina, and I was constantly worried it would break down in the middle of nowhere with no husband to call for help. It was the most unfun purchase ever, but at least I'll have something safe and reliable. I suppose I'll be judged for this, too, purchasing a car so soon after my husband died. I negotiated on the car, and I cried when the salesman gave me the keys. Tears of sadness, not joy. I sat there in the car...not a happy purchase at all. I'd been so worried about my car breaking down. Now I can take at least one thing off my list of things to stress about. Dealing with thank you notes, dinner, carpool—I'm exhausted and heartbroken.*

Went to my new book club at Dawn's house. Tried to have fun, but it's weird meeting people and having to tell them about myself. I felt the need to leave early. Took something to help me sleep. I love my kids. Woke up sad. My heart is sad. New day. New routine. New life, I guess.

Responding to an Author...

I decided to write Dr. Jennifer Ashton, to thank her for writing the book, *Life after Suicide*. I've never known anyone who died by suicide, and it's eerie how much I have in common with this woman.

January 7, 2020

Dear Dr. Ashton,

I never in a million years thought I'd be writing you this letter. I watch you on "Good Morning America" every morning, and yet, never thought we'd have so much in common. But I read your book, *Life After Suicide*, and as it turns out, we have a lot in common. I turn 50 in a few weeks. I, too, was married for 20-plus years. I was married to a doctor, an oncologist, named Matthew. We have teenage kids. Grady is 17, Gavin 15, and Sophie is 13. Our last family vacation was to Jamaica.

Our family recently relocated from Minneapolis, Minnesota to North Carolina for Matthew to join a small private practice. At first things seemed to be going well—until they weren't. Matthew, after only being with his new group for a few weeks, started to feel as if he'd made a "fatal mistake." He told me it was "career suicide," and he felt it was much like watching "a slow car crash." I told him he was being dramatic. I told him he should be grateful for all we had. I felt that I was brought to North Carolina for a reason. I kept saying, "Maybe God brought us all to the Bible Belt to get closer to Him, maybe you'll become a better doctor, maybe this will all work out for the best." Meanwhile, Matthew was slipping deeper and deeper into a depression.

Matthew was so full of life, and he lived his life to the fullest. His motto was, "We've gotta get it all in!" And he sure did pack a lot of living into his 49 years. We traveled the world, he loved to mountain bike, he took great pride in being a doctor, and felt it was an honor to treat cancer patients. We have a lake home in northern Minnesota that he dubbed, "my happy place." He enjoyed simple things, like grilling and doing lawn work. Most of all, he loved me and our three children…he loved us more than anything.

Matthew had been at his new job for only about three weeks when he realized it wasn't a good fit. He stopped sleeping, he stopped doing the things he enjoyed. I started journaling daily on October 27, 2019, as I became more and more concerned. I went to church on Saturday nights and Sunday mornings, and I prayed like I've never prayed before. After weeks of agonizing discussions with friends, our lawyer, my parents and his, we decided that Matthew had to quit his job. We all urged Matthew to go on anti-depressants, and to see a psychiatrist, but Matthew refused. He was a physician after all, and what would people think? He felt trapped by a noncompete in Minneapolis, where he longed to be, and by a two-year contract he'd signed with his new practice. Matthew just couldn't see a way out. At first, we hoped to get Grady (our senior) though the school year; then we moved the date to January 1, 2020. We brought Matthew to the emergency room on the evening of November 27, where they did not admit him. Matthew shot himself the next morning. It was November 28, 2019, Thanksgiving Day.

How can this be? My husband dedicated his life to saving lives, to helping those with cancer. My husband always chose life. I sit here still stunned and in shock as I write these words. How is this my life?

Dr. Ashton, I believe there is a story to be told here. Why is the physician suicide rate so high? Why don't people know more about this horrible disease? We need to destigmatize depression and mental illness for physicians. We need to help our physicians get the help *they* so desperately need without the fear of being fired, shunned or losing their medical licenses. The last place that my husband was—was a hospital. How ironic is that?

I feel I need to do something, something to raise awareness. And I don't know what that will be, but I do want to thank you for writing your book. It was hard to read, but in the end, it gave me hope. Hope not only for a brighter future for me and my kids, but hope that if we continue the conversation, we can prevent another suicide. It has shattered my family; my prayer is that it never shatters another.

Thanks so much for your words of wisdom. They were so helpful. I wish you and your family only the best.

With much love, gratitude, and warmest regards,

Betsy Gall

Yesterday I woke Grady up, or thought I did, yet he overslept. Crazy morning, went to the gym, home to shower, walk dog, and drop Soph at school. I've decided to remodel this house. It will be a nice distraction for me, and man, the house needs it.

Then back to the courthouse, which was not easy. Two and a half hours there, and still nothing accomplished. It's a joke watching this man with his thick coke bottle glasses perched on his nose, page through his big government book, trying to figure out how to help me. I feel like I could be on candid camera; however, it's not funny. It's frustrating and annoying that I need to do this.

Talked to kids about grief. Gavin was sitting in his room in the dark, looking at pictures of Matt on his phone. We go to see Gavin's therapist tonight, and I hope he is equipped for this because it's heavy. I worry about Sophie, my happy girl who never wants to be sad. This is awful. I miss Matt. It's been 41 days since I've seen him. Lord, I miss him. This is all so tragic.

- *Kindness of strangers*
- *Hugs from kids*
- *Sweet notes from neighbors*
- *Knowing calm will come someday*
- *Warmth in January*
- *Things to look forward to*

I'm looking forward to my walk with Missy. Kids have a half day of school today so I'm going to get some things done around the house.

- *Sunshine after rain*
- *Laughter from the next room over*
- *Happy daughter*

◎ *My dog in my bed*

Yesterday I met with two nurses who had formally left the North Carolina clinic—and had recently worked directly with Matthew. They loved and admired him. In only a short period of time they felt like they knew him—and knew him to be an excellent doctor. They wanted me to know how much they adored Matthew. This broke my heart because Matthew was loved by most everyone.

Please Lord, help me as I struggle with these questions of why, and these feelings of guilt. I feel sick, and I miss Matthew. I wasn't nice to him all the time; I feel awful and I feel as though it's my fault. But, on the other hand, as I put the pieces of the puzzle together, I have to ask, is this what was supposed to be? Was this God's plan? Why? I have several questions. My sweet, good-hearted husband is gone forever.

My kids now have no dad. I have no husband, and I'm left here all alone to raise them. How am I going to do it? Matthew loved us, and the healthy Matt Gall would never do this to us. My heart is shattered, and I am empty. Yesterday I wrote people more thank you notes.

It's 6 p.m., and I'm still processing everything from yesterday, including the visit with the nurses. Had to call one of Matt's buddies today, who went through the same depression thing recently. It's eerie that Matt tried to help his buddy with his depression—it's almost like foreshadowing was taking place. I still can't believe it. Talked to Matt's mom Elaine for an hour.

Gavin and I saw a license plate at church today that said James 1:2-3. I had to look it up: "Consider it pure joy, my brothers and sisters, whenever you face trials of many kinds, because you know that the testing of your faith produces perseverance." Oh Lord, help me consider this pure joy, not sure how to do that? How can you look at our situation and consider it pure joy?

Hmmm…so much to process. This is hard. I miss the music and I miss my old life where my problems were trivial. I'm sad— life is colorless, empty, and way too quiet. I believe being a doctor killed Matt. It was too stressful…it truly was the perfect storm.

Chapter 12
A Short Trip with Girlfriends

I was so lucky that my dear sister-in-law Diane stayed with my three teenagers so I could join my high school girlfriends on our annual girls' trip. It could not have come at a more perfect time.

January 23, 2020. I met Katie at the airport. She flew from LA to North Carolina, and we took the short flight to Grand Cayman together. We had talked on the plane about Matthew, which I'm still processing. She's good for me, so good for my soul. Katie has an amazing ability to live in the present. I have known Katie since day one of my life. Our parents are best friends, and we grew up across the street from each other. My kids love to hear stories about the childhood plays we would write and perform, as well as the shenanigans that we would pull back in our teenage days. We met the Minneapolis girls in Grand Cayman at the airport, arrived to our amazing 2700-sq.-ft. condo on the beach. Girls gave Debbie and me the master bedroom, it's beautiful. Went to the beach and drank wine. Went to the liquor store and bought more wine. Drank, ate pizza, talked, cried, and laughed. Bed early, we were all exhausted. Up at 4 a.m. and saw an email from Grady's math teacher. God does answer prayers—she had needed my note (and our tiny thank you gift) as much as we needed her. This is a good reminder that a little kindness can go a long way. Nobody knows what it is like to walk in another person's shoes. Gave the girls their presents last night, and they loved the flip flops and bracelets. Meg gave us monogrammed pajama bottoms. Katie gave face rollers and books for journaling. I love these girls. I ran five miles this morning, listening to my music. Went through some emails and notes and found a picture of Matt on St. Patrick's Day that my mom had been looking for. Matt loved every holiday, especially those celebrating beer and meat products. My mom and dad had Matthew over every St. Paddy's day because he was the only one that would eat corned beef and cabbage with my father. Back at the condo, I'm writing at the dining table with a view that is overlooking the dazzling Caribbean Sea. I must continue my list of things to be grateful for.

- *Aqua blue water*
- *Laughter with your besties, the best medicine*
- *Strong legs to run, and a heart to keep up*
- *Amazing views*
- *Worship music*
- *Flowers*

◎ *The beach*

God's beauty is everywhere! I now look at the sun, the bright aqua water, the white sand, and see how beautiful our world is. Thank you, God, for allowing me to take this time to soak up all of your beauty with my best friends. Yesterday, as we lay on the beach, Deb and I shared a taco, we read tabloid magazines and our book club books, we chatted nonstop, then we came up to the room for some rosé.

The girls and I talk about our lives. We get caught up on husbands and kids. We confide in each other. I can't help but feel that they are all lucky, and I am not. We went to Luca for dinner. Atmosphere was fun and festive.

Cutely dressed ladies sat next to us, and they were a hoot. Then a large party of beautiful people came in. They were loud and rambunctious and I thought, I want to be that…with Matthew and our friends. *We used to be that party. Back to the villa balcony where Katie, Beth, and I talked and talked and talked until almost 11 p.m., and I was tired. My heart aches, and I had to take sleep medication so I could fall asleep.*

Up at 7 a.m. today. Today I choose happiness. There is more sun to be soaked up today. I'm going to choose to make it a fabulous day.

◎ *Cheaters to read the small print*
◎ *Pink-striped towels*
◎ *Cabana boys who set up our chairs*

- *Palm trees*
- *Birds chirping*
- *Sailboats*
- *Phone calls from kids*

The trip changes the third day as Katie has to leave, which makes my heart sad. It's easy being with these girls from my childhood who know me this well. I cry at the drop of a hat. We sit and chat, and they've been understanding and patient with me over all these years with all of my problems, dealing with Grady's teenage issues as well as Matthew's challenges. Oh Lord, I know I shouldn't ask, but why me? These past few years have been awfully agonizing. I'm looking at the beautiful ocean with a gigantic cruise ship out there, and I ponder at the hugeness of it all. The hugeness of our lives, and then the small inner circle that can bring us such peace. I know I will be happy again. As a planner, it's odd because today, not knowing my next move does not stress me out. God has taken care of me. He has a plan for my life, I know it. I just keep repeating in my brain Jeremiah 29:11: "'For I know the plans I have for you,' declares the Lord, 'plans to prosper you and not to harm you, plans to give you hope and a future.'" But dang, again today my heart is over-whelmingly heavy.

We are planning on staying in tonight, which sounds perfect. Last night was the first night I didn't take anything to sleep. I tossed and turned a bit, which could have been all the food and wine we've been indulging in, but I feel pretty good—except for a sad, lonely, empty heart. Other than that, I'm grateful for all that I have. I've been a lucky, blessed girl all these years of my life.

Today is our last day in beautiful Grand Cayman. I had some happy moments, but I am sad. I'm excited to see the kids. Excited to get the house project going. I want to be with my family and know that they will be okay. I still can't believe it. My head swirls with images of Matt the morning he passed away. The months leading up to it seem so long ago now. This is aberrant. I didn't sleep well last night, maybe because my mind is on overdrive with all that I have to do. Lawyers, my real estate business, possibly moving back to Minnesota, registering kids for school, finding a place to live, and Grady going to college. It's overwhelming looking toward a completely different future. What is that future? I want happy, healthy kids, and I wonder if that will ever be possible? My mom, who has never been to North Carolina, comes to visit Wednesday through Monday to help me to make some decisions. I can't believe that this is my life. I have no husband. And the lake house, every inch of that place is him—all him and our dreams. Oh Lord, it's so awful. I don't want to leave Grand Cayman, yet I do.

I sat on a lounge chair on the white sandy beach just bawling my eyes out. The girls each laid a hand on me—but they didn't say a word. I told them to go home and hug their husbands, tell them that they love them. The girls had tears streaming down their cheeks, too. Everyone loved Matthew. They let me cry and get it all out. Being with the girls has been the best, but I miss my children. My heart feels as though it is being stabbed over and over again.

Chapter 13

Doing Things Alone...Without Matthew

I t's early February, and I didn't think much about watching the Super Bowl. But it turned out to be dreadful because I'm all alone, and Matthew absolutely loved to watch football. This was another event that snuck up on me and hit me like a punch to the gut that I wasn't expecting. There's a hole in my heart that's hemorrhaging. Yesterday a woman told me, "It's not fun to be a widow." Ummmm...thanks. I think I knew that. Life is difficult, and I think about how blessed I've been throughout my whole life, but it means nothing without Matt. Yes, the life insurance money is a gift, but as the pastor said yesterday, it runs through us and isn't even ours to begin with. Life insurance is so necessary but a truly heart-wrenching way to get money. Doing taxes yesterday sucked. I'm not sure which box to check: Taxpayer or spouse? I've always done most of the household chores and the finances on my own, but now it's truly only me doing everything, and I hate it. I can't sleep well, there is a bloody hole in my heart, and it sucks, and I can't think of any other way to describe it.

"Be still, and know that I am God; I will be exalted among nations, I will be exalted in the earth." Psalm 46:10. It's the verse that got me through selling my first real estate flip, which had been worrisome for me. I was anxious about the outpouring of money, and the time it is was taking, yet Matthew was very calm. He said, "It's not going to ruin us, Bets." That was so nice of him to say. That's when I started taking this Psalm verse seriously, as I'd become worked up over the financing of that little place. I was so stressed about getting it done in a timely fashion. Looking back, those were simple days and simple worries.

Last night at church we heard the story of a local family involved in a car accident that took two children from the most adorable couple ever, and it happened on their sixth wedding anniversary. The grief and pain they experienced was not freaking fair—it was way too much. How did they survive that loss? I think of Vanessa Bryant losing her husband, Kobe, and 13-year-old daughter, Gianna, on the same day. Why God? Why all of the suffering? I look at my kids and hope and pray that they will be okay. They are all processing things differently. I love them dearly.

Today I met with the attorney that will open Matthew's estate. I want this part to be over with.

⊚ Jennifer and her son, who have been such good friends to both Gavin and me

- *Missy and her silliness*
- *Reminders to "Be still and know that I am God"*
- *Simplicity*
- *Texts from my other sister-in-law*
- *Dimmers on light switches to help set the mood*

Oh Matthew, sweet man, oh how I miss you, even the annoying parts. Was it the concussions? You asked me that. "Do you think it's the concussions, Bets?" I said, "I don't know Matthew." I wish I'd told you how much I loved you the morning that you died. I am glad you knew it though. All of the texts I sent. I wanted to save you. I tried so hard. Oh Matthew, people move all the time. They change jobs. I had no idea it'd be that terrible and traumatic for you. I am incredibly sorry.

- *Memories of smiles*
- *Thinking about past vacations*
- *Inside jokes between the two of us*
- *Tears to get it all out*
- *Ears to hear God*
- *Dog kisses*

Sometimes I wake up afraid, which I did today, February 15. I can't believe I am on my own. We were watching videos on Matt's phone last night while waiting for some friends to come into town. There was one of Matthew and me skiing, kids whizzed pass us, and we laughed at the thought of going down the mogul-filled mountain. Matthew skied off, yelling to me, "I love you!" Yes! *I thought,* I got an I love you from Matthew on Valentine's Day after all. *Made me happy! I do hope to find true love again. I don't understand why I am even thinking this. Is it because Matt said, "You'll get remarried again"? I don't know but I do know that one has to have hope in order to go on.*

I talked to Matt's primary doctor yesterday. He said that Matthew's death was a punch to his gut, too, that Matthew never showed any signs of depression. He talked about how doctors think they can fix them-selves — that they can fix it all. Oh God, I wish I'd done more. I wish I'd known more *as the spouse of a physician.*

I'll look back someday with a smile because it was a beautiful life.

My boys are upset. They said that with Dad gone, "Everything is different now." Gavin told me that he has thoughts of throwing himself off a parking garage. Oh God, No! My heart sank as he cried and said he badly wants to go back to Minnesota. Psalm 30:5: "For his anger lasts only a moment, but his favor lasts a lifetime; weeping may stay for the night, but rejoicing comes in the morning." 2 Corinthians 4:17 "For our light and momentary troubles are achieving for us an eternal glory that far outweighs them all." Trials do serve a purpose, Lord, but what purpose will this serve my kids? Will they be okay? This is such a huge and heavy load to carry. Gavin was the closest to Matt. I love him so much, Lord. Please protect us and keep us safe. This is not fair. Matthew, I know you were sick, but this is not fair, what you did to us. I know deep down that this isn't your fault. What you left me with, though. Our hearts feel weighted, and I have lots to figure out. Our "new normal." What will it be? Thank you, Lord, for today. Thank you for my beautiful children.

- ◎ *Caffeine, it's a staple!*
- ◎ *Being able to be there for my kids*
- ◎ *Hugs*
- ◎ *Prayers from others, I can feel them*
- ◎ *Friends that visit*
- ◎ *Knowing that time will heal*

It's been a tough few days. I'm feeling unsettled as I wrestle with the decision to move back to Minnesota, but it has to be. I've got to put the kids first, and as Soph said, the snow, the gloomy weather, "It's just home, Mom." My girlfriends have been amazing, stating they'll come down again and help with the packing. Joe, the contractor, came by yesterday, and we've scaled back the project but I'll still do the kitchen, as well as Sophie and Grady's bathrooms. Maybe mine, too, we will see. The entire house needs new windows, and I am going to do the pool.

I have to, it was a promise that we made to the kids, and it's one I plan to keep.

Kids have been a little better lately. Grady shaved some of his eyebrow to make him look "tough." This scares me. I wish he'd find some inner peace. His therapist said he cried a lot in therapy. He misses Matthew. We all do. Matthew was larger than life.

It's February 26, 2020—after barely sleeping, I'm up, and I just read my devotional book. It talks about God leading us through our lives. Our futures feel flimsy—even precarious. That is how God wants it to be so we can rely on Him. Secret things belong to God, and future things are secret things.

Amazing to me that it is exactly what I needed to read today—I need to stop stressing so much. We will find the perfect place to land in Minnesota. I will be okay. I will find well-qualified, good renters for this house because I love it, and I'm not ready to sell it. My husband died here; I am keeping the house. I love my job, and it will provide me with a good income. I will spread awareness about physician suicide, and I will be happy and whole again. I will believe, and I am going to refuse to let anyone steal my joy or excitement or my love and passion for life.

Three months ago today our world changed, but it seems like forever ago. My Minnesota girlfriends arrived yesterday. They came back again to help me. I am so lucky to have them. We walked, had lunch, picked up Gav and Soph from school, then had wine and dinner out with the children. Sophie left dinner when she was finished. I looked over and the boys were laughing. And then they weren't. Gavin finished dinner; Grady had not. Gavin wanted to leave as he had three exams to study for. Grady was pissed that he was abandoning him. This led to a very long conversation with Grady about forgiveness. He is such a caring, sensitive soul, yet he wants to be tough. I do worry about him. Grady wishes he had received the University of Wyoming acceptance letter a day earlier—thinking maybe that could have saved his dad. I had to explain that it wouldn't have. Matt got sick…it was like getting cancer. We're going to need some family therapy. Grady is leaving soon, and I want us all to be on good terms. I wish that he would do more to help himself, though. He is quick to blame, judge, and hold a grudge—all of Matthew's and my bad traits. I hope and pray that he can work through his feelings.

Today we start to organize and sort through Matthew's stuff. Not sure if I can do Matthew's closet. I took my wedding ring off because I am so mad that I have to do this. I love my ring, which is a culmination of three stones, two of which were an addition for my 40th birthday, and two bands. It represented the five of us. Now we are a family of four. I can no longer look at this ring as it's a reminder that he abandoned me. I'm praying the disgusting hot tub in the backyard gets picked up today and that our landscaper can help with redesigning the overgrown and horrendous backyard. It looks awful back there, and I want it to get done.

I pray for my financial advisors, and my estate attorneys, I pray that they may all have our best interests at heart. It's good having my girlfriends here, and I already hate to think about them leaving. Thank you, God, for my beautiful life. Things could be so much worse. If I had to worry about putting food on the table or if I had a sick child, I don't know how I would manage. Please help me find the right words to guide my children.

Yesterday was hard. My friends helped me go through Matthew's clothes and some stuff in the garage. We took two loads to Goodwill. Grief hits you, like when I found the ads and promo pieces from The Group, Matt's Minnesota employer. Matt was smart; he had all that knowledge up there in that brain of his. Still can't believe he's gone. Still can't believe he took his own life. Lots of running around yesterday. Sophie made the track team. A friend texted me that she was "wicked" fast! That's my girl. I'm extremely proud of her. House was filled with kids last night, which I loved. Got a little boozy with the girlfriends.

I woke up with anxiety again today. I'm fighting a cold and didn't sleep well. Going to the country club with a friend tonight and will be home early and I won't drink as much. Going to do a family session with our therapist tomorrow, which I'm looking forward to. Then, we're having Chris and Di over for dinner. The landscaper is coming to look at the yard again today. I was bummed they didn't take the hot tub yesterday because it's a mess back there. It'd be easier to stay and put the pool in while I am here. I want to make it beautiful, but now I'm (sort of) looking forward to moving home. I'll miss buds on the trees and green grass in February, but I'll love being by my family and my Minnesota girlfriends. My life has been so beautiful, and I'm feeling blessed beyond belief. Everything will work out; it'll all fall into place. I'm lucky to have such good friends and family. I want to do something good for someone today. Breathe, peace, love—God is good!

Early March 2020, the coronavirus is rearing its ugly head and making people crazy. People are stocking up on bottled water. I'm trying not to watch the news; I just pray that God will protect my family. I've had a vision of a wedding on the beach. I think it's me in the wedding. Not sure though. It's been only six months since Matt's death, and I know thoughts of a wedding are too soon, and I don't really understand these images. Then I remembered Matt's last word to me were: "You are going to get married again." Maybe Matt was sending me messages in my dreams and to my subconscious that he wanted me to be happy again. I think that Matt was giving me hope for my future, but I don't know if I ever want to get married again. Time will tell.

I'm also thinking about a pretty house in Edina. Not sure why? I'm reading The Body Keeps The Score; *it is about the brain, mind, and body in the healing of trauma. It's intense and not an easy read for me. I talked to Grady about maybe trying to exercise and get a job. He's been sweet, but it's the video games and smoking pot that worries me a lot. I have to fly solo now with this parenting gig, and it's challenging. Matt really loved the kids, and recently he wasn't himself. The old Matt Gall would have never done something like this. I can't comprehend it—and I hope nobody else has to ever go through it.*

I prayed this morning for all of my children, friends, and family. I prayed over our future. I am blessed and grateful. I know things will fall into place. I just finished the book Turn Mourning into Dancing, *by Henri Nouwen. He writes about facing not only our own deaths, but willingly allowing for the deaths of those we know and love and live with. Dying comes as a condition of life, and therefore a condition for Christian growth. Thinking about this reminds me that life is precious.*

Tonight was good with the kids. After Gavin and I had a therapy session with his therapist, we went out to dinner. Sophie was with her boyfriend. He's adorable, by the way, and I think this kid is going to stick around for a while. Kids had a half day of school. I'm tired of thinking about next steps. I'm tired of thinking about everything. Life is peculiar. I sometimes feel like my feet are in mud, but I keep putting one foot in front of the other. Stuff is getting done, and we are moving forward, slowly but surely. This still feels like I am in a nightmare of a movie, and unfortunately, I am playing the lead role.

I keep thinking about the discovery with our therapist last Sunday. Grady's door was locked the morning his dad came to it to give him a hug goodbye. I thought Grady felt bad that he didn't get his one last hug goodbye—but he was or is upset because he knows or thinks that he would have had the where-withal to stop Matthew. So, I wonder about God's will. Was this the way Matthew was supposed to die? I guess God gives us free will…it has to be, because how else can it be explained? It's hard not to think about this all of the time. The therapist also told me that Matthew had already disconnected the morning he died — he was detached, and that was why he told me I'd get married again. This makes sense, I guess.

Grady's therapist said I was doing an amazing job, and while I think "amazing" is a strong word, I know that I am doing the best that I can. I love these kids so much. Grady had a dream that Matthew was in a mental institution. Matt would never have wanted that. It's all clear to me now that there is a master plan — God has the plan, and it's all figured out. Maybe Matthew lived his 49 years to his fullest because it was going to be short. He was full of life, unique and smart, driven — but the stress that man had to deal with simply became too much. It's all clear to me, as every book I read on suicide references the perfect storm. We had a perfect storm.

That being said, there is a story to be told: we need our doctors to be healthy, and we need to get this story out there. Doctors are part of an exclusive club and not easily replaced. They shouldn't be required to have all of the answers all of the time. The stress is too much.

- ◎ *Walks with the girls*
- ◎ *Pizza with the family*
- ◎ *Future trips planned*
- ◎ *Andrew, who has been my Uber driver*

Psalm 37:3-4: "Trust in the Lord and do good; dwell in the land and enjoy safe pasture. Take delight in the Lord, and he will give you the desires of your heart." What a passage this is! I have hope about my future, with much to look forward to. It's odd to wake up each morning and feel blah, colorless, and dull. This is grief, I guess. I wake up with a thud, blah. It's such an icky feeling, and I hate it. I used to wake up filled with energy and joy. Wow, how quickly things can change. Yesterday was busy, and I was having a good day until I saw a picture of Matthew; then my heart sank again. My darling husband. Oh Matthew, I love you. We had such a beautiful life together. You made it exciting. The silence around here can be deafening, and I hate it.

God is good. My life is surrounded by several beautiful, sweet, and kind people.

I think I saw three Steelers signs—the Pittsburgh Steelers were Matthew's favorite football team—so I must have seen "signs" from Matthew yesterday. I used to be so annoyed with Matthew's passion for the Steelers. He would, as a forty-year-old man, "decorate" the basement for every single game. He'd have Steelers blankets and helmets placed all around. He'd sit down there on the sofa with his cold beer in his Steelers mug and scream (or cheer), depending on the team's winning or losing status. The kids joke that this is how they learned all of the world's best swear words.

It's been a few months now, but I looked up Matthew's **Minneapolis Star Tribune** *obituary, and sure enough, another patient has written a comment: "My family would like to extend* *our deepest sympathy to the family of Dr. Gall. We just learned of his passing and are saddened to hear this news. We met Dr. Gall in January of 2019 when my father was referred to him. His infectious personality and joy of life came through bright and clear during our conversations of treatment plans and subsequent follow-up sessions. He always had a smile to share and a listening ear. Prayers for peace and comfort to you all."*

Daylight savings started March 8. I'm at the airport at 8:30 for an early morning flight to Minneapolis. Didn't sleep well because I was nervous about the time change, leaving the kids, and the big decision before us. I thought yesterday about my final conversation with Matthew, one I don't like to think about. He said, "Do you think it was the concussions?" I told him he had mental illness, and he accepted that answer.

How did this happen to us, Lord? Will I ever have answers? Does it even matter? Or do we make it up to help ourselves feel better? God, please show me the way, show me the light. Help me God, and keep my family safe. Thank you, God, for all that you've given me.

- ◎ *Reading good books*
- ◎ *Airplanes already at the gate*
- ◎ *Places to go*
- ◎ *People waiting for you*

Psalm 18:30: "As for God, his way is perfect: The Lord's word is flawless; he shields all who take refuge in him." Matt's mother told one of his "best friends" that Matthew made everyone feel as though they were Matthew's best friend. That didn't sit well with this guy, but she's right, Matt did make everyone feel that way. Secretly, I know that Matt was my best friend. He told me everything. Well, except that he was going to kill himself.

I guess we could move back here to Minnesota and be fine. Yesterday's weather was so dreary, but I'll get used to it again. This coronavirus is out of control, people are freaking out, markets are nuts… I'm not listening. I'm tuning it out as I can't take the stress. I can't live with the toxicity, so I've turned it over to God. And a friend said yesterday, "He's got you." I believe He does. Almost everyone that God places into my life has such an undeniable faith. It sure does help to be on the same page with most people.

John 16:33: "I have told you these things, so that in me you may have peace. In this world you will have trouble. But take heart! I have overcome the world." Lord, the world is in mass-panic mode right now. All hell has broken loose with coronavirus. My grocery store was packed today, yet the shelves were bare. The feeling of being all alone now to deal with the coronavirus is inconceivable to me. Lord, please keep my family safe. I wish people would read more of the Bible so that they could feel the peace of God's love. Track and volleyball have been canceled indefinitely. Not sure if the boys can go back to Minneapolis next weekend. It's crazy and a bit scary, but I know we will all be okay. My kids will not get sick.

Attended Bible study yesterday and was overcome with grief and tears. I love that sweet church and those ladies there. We stood up to sing, and I could barely hold myself up with the tears flowing like water—I miss my sweet Matthew. I have a vision of him smiling down upon me. But, to be left here alone to raise these kids is an unimaginable responsibility. I canceled my lunch with Amanda and came home. She's awesome, but I'm exhausted and couldn't do it. I made a big pile of my paperwork, made a sandwich, and sat outside in the sunshine to work. I called my parents, sent an email to the estate lawyer, and worked on pool plans. When Grady came and asked me to go with him to take Liberty for a walk, I dropped everything to be with him.

"When I am afraid, I put my trust in you." Psalm 56:3. Why did I start reading the Bible so late? Many good verses teaching ways to live our lives are in this great book. Right now, in this moment, I need peace. Lord, give me peace and protect my family.

Can't sleep. Had a pretty awful day yesterday. Weather turned cold again, and it was cloudy. I ran, walked, and prayed for an hour in my beautiful neighborhood—missing Matt immeasurably. Came back and watched the news for 30 minutes, which is about all I can take. Then I watched online church. Found an envelope Matt had in his desk full of cards from patients, such sweet cards with kind notes. Matthew kept every card a patient ever gave him, and I found at least a hundred. He touched thousands of lives. People need to thank their doctors more often. Reading the cards made me bawl my eyes out. I couldn't stop crying. I ask why? Why is this my life? Talked to the kids, gave a coronavirus update, and told them they'd be starting online school tomorrow.

Dear Lord, please give me peace. Psalm 36:7-9. Psalm 132:15. John 6:12-13. Loved pastor's sermon yesterday. I need to figure out how to be more of a blessing to others during these turbulent times. Thank you, God, for today. Please use me wisely, guide my words and my actions. I love you God. I keep envisioning me on a rowboat with Jesus, my head rests upon his shoulder, and we are in calm waters.

Woke up after having a dream of someone coughing on my food. Coronavirus has crept into my dreams now. People are asking me what Matthew would have thought about the coronavirus—and I have no idea. I try not to spend too much time thinking about improbable situations. It's a waste of time.

I lie in bed and think of my old life. I think of the summer days playing with my kids on the front lawn in Minnesota— waiting for Matthew to drive up the street, on his way home from work in his black SUV, sunglasses and a smile on his face— finally home after a long day of work. The kids jump up and down, so excited to see him. I kiss him on the lips, then head inside to start dinner. Oh, how I miss those simpler days.

- *My children safe and sound in their beds*
- *Happy memories of Matthew*
- *Springtime, which gives me hope*
- *Zoom happy hour with besties*

- *Cell phones*
- *The Xbox – who knew that I'd be happy for this one day!?*
- *Old friends who can read you like a book*
- *Food in the pantry*
- *TVs that work*
- *A beautiful neighborhood*

Hebrews 12:28-29: "Therefore, since we are receiving a kingdom that cannot be shaken, let us be thankful, and so worship God acceptably with reverence and awe, for our God is a consuming fire." Huh, so I have to think about that one!?? I wake up every day, and I am thankful for my life, my family, my kids, our God, and our health—we've been blessed beyond belief. Yesterday, due to the coronavirus spread, we got orders to shelter in place through April 16—that's 22 days! Yes, I can do these 22 unexpected days with my kids—without friends over or family coming to visit for spring break. I'm sad that Grady won't have a graduation ceremony, that kid can't catch a break, but I'm happy that I get this extra time with him (even though I hate some of his choices). So, yesterday, I ran and walked but today...I have to really run hard today. It was a cloudy, dreary day. I met with the kids to give them an update on the state of our world. The virus has slowed in South Korea and China, but Italy has taken a hard hit, along with Spain, and now we brace for the raging coronavirus storm to hit America. One in 1,000

New Yorkers have the virus. And unfortunately, our Maui spring break is canceled.

I am so happy that we were able to have a funeral for Matthew. I feel bad for the thousands of people who don't get that same opportunity for closure.

My high school boyfriend, Scot, died 28 years ago today on April 30. 2 Corinthians 4:18: "So we fix our eyes not on what is seen, but on what is unseen, since what is seen is temporary, but what is unseen is eternal." Hmmm, lots to unpack with that. Focus on the unseen, which is what I'm choosing to do. The good that will come out of Matt's death, the good that will come out of this pandemic; it will be good. Someday.

Actually, if I'm going to help spread awareness of doctors and stress—it couldn't be at a better time. As we face this healthcare crisis right now, our doctors and nurses are under an enormous amount of stress. They are going to need love, prayers, and we need to change the system for them. Doctors are thought to have all of the answers, but they are people, smart people, and we NEED them—we need healthy doctors.

We want to get back to Minnesota now that we've made our decision to move. The unknowns are tough, but I'm not in charge. Patience is a virtue, and I promise and pray, but at the end of the day, it's on God's timeline. Patience has never been my strong suit.

Palm Sunday was yesterday; Holy Week is upon us. I'm clueless about the Bible and the stories of the Lord, so this is my year to learn more. Grady's 18th birthday yesterday was hard, *which caught me off guard. I sobbed behind my sunglasses as he opened his gifts. Then he read the letter I wrote him, word for word, and gave me a heartfelt thank you. I took a picture of the letter so that I'll always remember this moment in time. He is such a sweet guy, and I can't imagine having endured what he has when I was that age. It was a pretty nice day.*

- ⊚ *Flowers blooming in April*
- ⊚ *Mondays – the start of a new week means we're one week closer to this pandemic being over*
- ⊚ *Text messages*
- ⊚ *Toilet paper!*
- ⊚ *Birds chirping*
- ⊚ *Routines – they help*
- ⊚ *A simple wave from people as I go on my runs*
- ⊚ *Liberty's groans and funny ways*
- ⊚ *Sun rising over the lake*
- ⊚ *Beautiful North Carolina architecture*
- ⊚ *The way Grady is listening to our prayers*
- ⊚ *Umbrellas for shade*
- ⊚ *Green grass*

Now, months later, I think back to the morning Matt died— and I can't help but go over it a million times. I was exhausted and scared—and wanted him to get in the car. How long did I sit in my car? I wrote a note telling the kids we were going to the hospital. Matt's last words were, "Will there be sirens?" He

The Illusion of the Perfect Profession • 189

said "Do you think it was the concussions?" "Oh Matthew,
sweetie, I don't know. Let's go!" He looked cute in a white t-
shirt and glasses. He was a good man. Why? Why did his brain
go so sour? Could it have been prevented? I know he loved us. I
feel like I lost him in early September, having visions of him sit-
ting in the office staring at the computer. Lord, I think about his
patients. How are they dealing with this? Why didn't Matt lis-
ten to me? He had texted me, "What's wrong with my brain?"
He thought he shouldn't put some things in text. Was it para-
noia? Or was it the truth?

- *Cynda said the nicest thing: She said that I didn't have the power to stop Matthew*
- *Cuteness of pets — Winston and Liberty's play dates*
- *Sophie asking me to polish her nails*
- *Approved for a mortgage, even though I have no income*
- *Signs of hope*

Yesterday I volunteered to pack lunches at the local high
school. I thought about all those 200-plus kids getting this
food—they have no other way because of this pandemic. I took a
walk when I got back home because it was a picture-perfect day.
Sunny and 80 °F! I love the weather in North Carolina. It's cur-
rently snowing in Minnesota. I listened to Grace Like a Flood
Part 4—about how we are already saved. Interesting. I wish
Grady would learn more about God, and I need him to know it's
not always about religion, but the goodness of God. Talked with

a counselor in Minnesota because I need to get all of us set up with therapists—good ones. I've been having wild dreams that leave me unsettled in the morning. At least I'm sleeping hard enough that I'm dreaming.

I'm going to try and listen better to the Lord—how can I be of service? How can I be a blessing to others? At book club last night, after we went around and each of us told about what was going on in our lives—people told me that it was okay for me to be sad or mad. I find it annoying that people tell me that. I don't need permission for my feelings. Do I need to "prove" to people that I'm sad? That I wake up not as my former "happy" self? My life has been altered forever, and I have been broken, I've had my heart stomped on, more than once. I choose to look at the bright side of life. I'm choosing to be grateful. I'm choosing light over darkness; I'm choosing good over evil. Suicide makes you feel like you can't or shouldn't ever be happy again. That's bullshit, and it's not fair. I'm choosing God as my savior, and that feels a whole lot better than the alternative. Of course, my old comfortable life was nice, but it wasn't easy all the time. There were tough sides to my marriage; I could get really annoyed with Matt at times. His need for perfectionism was difficult to deal with. This is my life now. There is no turning back the clock, and it's pointless to think about that.

- ◎ *A nod and a smile from a stranger*
- ◎ *Talks with Megan, she's my person*
- ◎ *Cynda and our walks*

- *Sparkling blue lake*
- *Hope – it's so important, what would I do without it?*
- *Routines*
- *"Comfys." These giant, oversized hoodies arrived today without a note, and I wonder—who sent us these? There are four of them, and they are amazing!*

I dropped an exercise weight on Matt's beloved vintage car and dented it. I'm working out in the garage because my gym is closed due to coronavirus. Matthew would be so unbelievably mad at me if he saw this. He cherished that car. I'm tired, Lord. In 10 days, it'll be five months since he died. What will my life look like in this next phase, Lord? How do I write a book? Help me use my voice, Lord, for good. There are many moving pieces. Thank you, God, for my children, and Chris, Di, and Andrew.

I'm thinking we will leave before May 15 now. Next week more contractors will be working on the house. My outside space will be invaded, and with people working here, it'll be different, so we need to get out of their way. Therefore, for now I'll concentrate on packing up the house. I miss Matthew and our partnership. Being at the lake will be difficult this summer; I can barely think about being there without him. It really was his happy place, and it was the only place where he could truly relax. Well, he'd relax after all the chores were done, kids had tubed and skied and the lawn was perfect.

- *A good Netflix series*

- *Smell of suntan lotion*
- *A good book*
- *Hopeful texts from strangers*
- *Liberty's big brown eyes*
- *I say this one so often: sunshine.*

April 26, 2020. We're leaving in one week for Minnesota. Our lives will never be the same. The four of us, my kids and me together in this house — living here as our primary residence — it's coming to an end, and I'm sad about that. What's wrong with me? I'm just sad. Sad to be leaving this chapter of my life — here in this cocoon with my kids all day and night. It feels safe being away from dealing with other people's grief. I like it here in North Carolina — I love it actually — and this is my home. My friends here aren't grieving Matthew — now I have to go back to that. I need my friend Wendy. I need to ask her how she did life without her husband, without caring about being judged. I know people will look at me differently. I do not want to go back, but I am doing it for my kids.

- *God*
- *Quiet mornings after the storm*
- *A clean doggie*
- *College bestie Sarah*
- *My dad*
- *My brothers*

- *I'm grateful that my brother and sister-in-law bought a boat, and I hope it'll bring their family happiness and joy and togetherness and healing*
- *Diane, she's always there for me*
- *Stupid housewives TV shows that take my mind off of my pain*
- *My six-mile runs in the neighborhood*
- *Dreams — at least we can always dream*
- *Business — to keep my mind off of my life*
- *Memories of happier days*
- *I know I say this all the time, but birds singing*
- *Today, the scale headed in the right direction*
- *Being able to check things off my list*
- *My nephew Andrew, who is always helpful. My car battery died, and he fixed it right away*
- *Texts from Di. She keeps sending them, and I love her for it*
- *My children's friends, they bring my kids joy, therefore they bring me joy, and I love them all*

Chapter 14
Return to Live in Minnesota

May 2, 2020: Today is the day we leave this chapter behind, and I can't stop crying.

Dearest Matt,

We're going home today. You would have loved that, wouldn't you of? Going to live at the lake again this summer. Matthew, I thought about what a gift it was that last summer we had a whole month at the lake. I'll never forget our walks to the mailbox and our talks on the boat about our future. Life sure was different back then. I know I have your blessing, to go on, to be happy again.

You were a sweet man, a great doctor, a really good dad, and we all know how much you loved us. I'll try my best to do this without you, I really will. I'll keep your memory alive, I'll teach the kids about love, and faith, and the importance of the little things. I'll remind them of your love for each of them and stress the importance of education. I'll tell them to be generous and compassionate with both their time and resources. I'll teach them and don't worry; God and I have got your back.

Thanks, Matthew Gall, for those kids—they're simply the best. I promise to do the best job that I can. I hope you are having fun up in heaven, and I'll see you there someday.

Love you always and forever,

~B.

- Vendors to call when things go wrong
- Texts from Grady
- "I love yous" from Sophie
- Gavin's awesomeness and helpfulness
- Car to get me from here to there
- Wine. I'm drinking too much of it, but it dulls the constant pain
- Memories of a happier time

May 11, 2020. We've been living at the lake house for almost a week now. It's been excruciatingly difficult for me, but on the flip side, oddly it has been soothing, too. I've finally been able to release what I knew was deep inside, but for whatever reason, couldn't connect with in North Carolina. I literally break down in hysterical tears while running. I have to stop moving in order to catch my breath and stop the sobs. It was almost like Matthew was never in North Carolina—he wasn't able to even give it a chance. Coming here to the lake house, and

facing Matthew's life head on, has been hard, yet sweet and ca-
thartic. He had saved every card and note from me. I didn't re-
member writing some of them let alone remember that he saved
them. Going through them was like opening up a sunken treas-
ure box. It reminded me of our early days, the good and simple
days. We were head over heels in love, it was fun to read those
cards.

Matt was extremely dedicated to his job and loved being a
doctor. Matt had to mask his pain because dealing with cancer
patients 24/7 is tough. His heart was too big. He was too good
of a person. He loved what he did, and that was who he was. He
was always a doctor before he was my husband, he was a doctor
before he was a father. It was a calling for him. At the end of his
life, he said he didn't think he could do it anymore, so of course
he became depressed. It hit him hard. But Matthew lived hard,
so looking back now it's no surprise to me that if Matthew was
going to get depressed, it would hit him harder than most. He
was so, so, so passionate. It was apparent at an early age how
different he was. Maybe God led him to live life to the fullest
because it was going to be a short one for him? It's still mind-
boggling to me that he is gone.

- ◎ *Kids' friends*
- ◎ *Zoom calls*
- ◎ *Sophie, even when she's mad at me*

Yesterday I started house hunting in Edina, the Minneapolis suburb where I was born. I never thought that the first house we saw in my childhood neighborhood would steal my heart. I love the fact that the kids loved it with all of its old 1928 Mediterranean charm. It delighted me that they thought it was cool. It would be like "coming home," coming full circle if we were to get it. It needs love, and I'd have to spend some dough on it, but I know I'd get my money back. I always long for projects to do—now I'd have two distractions to help me cope with my grief.

I saw my friend Wendy after the house hunt, and I really love that girl—she is hope for me. We have similar stories: both have three kids and lost our husbands at a young age. She's adorable, and so is her new husband. It will be nice having "built-in" friends when I get back to the Twin Cities. I'll have to take the "I don't give a damn" stance about what people think about me or my situation. I can't become overwhelmed because when I start to think of all I have to do, I get scared. A move, two major simultaneous renovation projects, writing a book, teenagers, starting my real estate business up again—sometimes I feel crushed by the thought of it all. But God says in the Bible, when we are weak, He is strong. I know I am strong. Inside and out. I nailed six miles on the treadmill yesterday. I am not only physically fit but mentally capable. I will look at these houses as my business, and we will use the North Carolina house as a rental. Because patience is not my virtue, I need to learn to be patient. It will all work out the way it was supposed to, Betsy. God is in charge, and I am thankful for all He has provided. I'm going to buy flowers today. Can't wait to bring some life up here to the lake. Hopefully the sun will come out and shine, which really helps.

Exodus 14:14: "The Lord will fight for you; you only need to be still."

John 14:27: "Peace I leave with you; my peace I give you. I do not give to you as the world gives. Do not let your hearts be troubled and do not be afraid."

Romans 8:28: "And we know that in all things God works for the good of those who love him, who have been called according to his purpose."

Yesterday, on my run, I listened to the last part of our nine-part series on Grace. Cynda is good at keeping me on my faith track. Thank you, God, for putting Cynda in my life...I owe it all to you. God has a plan for me. The plan is for good, I know He is taking care of me, and I know He will take care of me and my family for the rest of our lives.

- ◉ Author Mark Batterson's books
- ◉ FaceTime. Saw and talked to Grady last night on my phone
- ◉ Sibling love

May 30, 2020. I'm back in North Carolina visiting, and "Minneapolis is burning after riots." Frightened, Megan texted at 1:00 a.m. that she could hear "fireworks." I'm scared to go back there now. Thank the Lord for our lake house nestled in the *woods far away from the city. Grady is there and safe. I can't even imagine it. Watching the news, this seems both atrocious and unreal—it's completely devastating. Dear God, it feels as if the whole world is falling apart. I know I live in a bubble. I like my bubble. I wish that there was no racism, I wish that life was fair. I truly feel that because of the lack of God in people's lives, this is where we now are. Please God, I pray for peace. This is an awful time in history, truly devastating. I want my family together, I want calm. I want peace. God must become the center of my life. We need you, God, we need you now. The Bible says, "Be still and know that I am God."*

It feels as if the world is coming to an end. My dear Lord, why? Why the pain, suffering, murder, and destruction? Why all of the hate? Is it because we've strayed from you? The stress that I'm feeling is staggering. I'm scared and anxious. I feel powerless; we are all powerless. I am sick to my stomach, and my heart aches for this country. I miss Matthew, and my heart is simply shattered right now. I don't know what to do. Do I stay here? Do I try and go back? My life feels unraveled and frail. Life, you've really thrown me some curve balls.

- ◉ *Spectacular weather*
- ◉ *Peaceful protests*
- ◉ *Sunsets on the veranda*
- ◉ *Good uncles*
- ◉ *The Bible*

In June, I'm happy that we're past the six month's mark of Matt's passing because I do believe that time heals. I sometimes stop and can't believe or understand why this is my life. I had such a beautiful life before. There will always be a before and after the suicide now. I get mad that Matthew left us. A pandemic? Now riots and unrest? These are frightening times, and I'm doing it all alone. I'm lucky that I truly am not alone. God is our refuge and strength, an ever-present help in trouble. I need to be focused on Him and not be anxious about anything. It feels like the wheels are coming off the bus, but as Proverbs 31:25 says, "She is clothed with strength and dignity; she can laugh at the days to come." Thank you, Lord, for getting Sophie and me safely back to Minnesota. Thank you, for watching over all of us.

- Letting go
- Ears to listen to the kids
- Dinner with Grady and Soph
- Sun shining over the bunk house
- Cousins sleeping over
- TJ's funny words
- Girls laughing

I can't believe it's already June 9th. It was 95 degrees here yesterday. Soph and I got the place ready for the North Carolina kids who are arriving today. I feel lucky that my kids have such wonderful friends. Loads of things are going on. I had another heart-to-heart with Grady, and he is still so angry. And then Gav came upstairs, and he was crying, missing his dad. I rubbed his back as he said how Dad was so good at entertaining and was the fun guy at the lake. I told him that I'd been feeling the same way, the same pressure. This is tough. Sophie played a few videos yesterday, and hearing Matthew's voice again put me into tears.

I'll never fully understand how Matt's entire identity was being a doctor; it was who he was to the core—and at the end of his life he thought he couldn't do it anymore. I'll never understand the depth on the clinical side of why he didn't feel as though he could perform anymore. I always thought that being a doctor was a job, but it was so much more to him than that.

After I got Gavin settled down, he and Grady talked things out. Right now, Grady's a loose cannon—not uncommon in a teen. But dammit, I need to get him to college in Wyoming. Please God, let him go there to turn his life around. Please find him, let him seek you. Please Lord, help Grady. Help all of my children. Sweet Sophie lay in bed with me last night, telling me that I'm pretty and that I've done a good job as a mom. She truly is the best. Lord, please guide me with my words of wisdom, please soften their hearts and guide them thoughtfully through their grief. Thank you, God, for another beautiful morning.

◎ Surviving the night—having all these teenagers up here is stressful, but I'm grateful for them

- *My dad for meeting me halfway in Zimmerman, cutting my drive time in half*
- *Meaningful conversation with my mom*
- *Strength to power on*
- *The gym opens tomorrow — I can hardly wait to get back to normal!*

We're leaving the lake house for Minneapolis in an hour, and I still have lots to do. I'm crispy, and need a break from the sun. I have had fun with these kids. Gav starts football today. We're staying at a hotel in Edina, and I have a few appointments. Yesterday, I got boys off (after more cooking!), mowed the lawn, cleaned the bunk house, did 10 loads of laundry, talked to Matthew's mother, Elaine, and organized a bit of the garage. Matthew had like a hundred pairs of work gloves and a lot of bug spray. Well, now it's all organized. It made me sad being by myself on a Sunday afternoon. The kids were on the boat, and I'll now need to find ways to keep busy on the weekends.

June 25, 2020. Closing day of my new Edina home brings dread. Megan won't even be there because of dang Covid. Zephaniah 3:17: "The Lord your God is with you, the Mighty Warrior who saves. He will take great delight in you; in his love he will no longer rebuke you, but will rejoice over you with singing."

Dear God, I am imperfect. I'm anxious, I still try to control my mind from going in a thousand different directions. I miss Matthew, and I really don't like being back here in Minnesota at all. It's all for Gavin. Gavin deserves it, and what do I do? I yell at him last night for no reason. All I can think about is I'm a single mom, one person, and how do I do this all? I'm so unhappy, which is not in my nature. I have to fake it and pretend, but I'll keep putting one foot in front of the other. Please Lord guide me, help me make the right decisions. Help me hold my tongue, help me raise these kids right, make me a better person, show me the way, Lord, please show me the way.

A beautiful weekend here back at the lake house. Tomorrow we move into our new Edina house, and I will have tons to do, but I will enjoy today. God is with me, He is for me, He loves me! I'll continue on my path of listening to His whispers.

We are in the Edina house at the end of June. I'm frozen, having only a thin bed sheet because I can't find any blankets. I love this house; it's charming and inviting. I am going to make it our dream house by making it a happy house. I've always believed that your home is the backdrop to your life, so why not make it beautiful? I walked Liberty last night, and I still can't believe I live here in the neighborhood where I grew up. This morning while the thunder roars outside, I read one of my daily devotionals, in which the author talks about overcoming: Child of God, you may be suffering, but you can't fail if you only dare to believe, stand tall, and refuse to be overcome. I must power on.

I finished my letter to Matt for his July 9th birthday party. It wasn't easy, but I got through it. The kids and I worked again on cleaning out the garage at the lake, and we're getting there. Dang, Matthew had so much stuff.

Matthew loved every holiday, but especially the July 4th holiday. Another one that will never be the same without him. The kids did a great job decorating the lake house just like Matthew would have done if he'd been here. Oh Matthew. (I say this all the time silently to myself, Oh Matthew.) Yesterday I came up with the idea of the white balloons for his birthday. I'm excited about that. On the boat, the kids and I can spread his ashes over the lake he so loved, and every guest will let go of a balloon at the same time. Oh Matthew. I talked to Elaine yesterday. I asked her since God is love, did evil win? She's struggling with that one too—which is good for me to know because she is a believer, and has been for much longer than me. Mom and Dad arrived about 1:30 p.m. We had lunch and then the kids and I went on the boat. It was a perfect hot summer day. My darling niece, Emmy, slept over. I watched them out on the boat after dinner, then watched them swimming and jumping off the dock. It was the best. They already have the best memories of this place, and I pray they continue forever. My kids are amazing humans. These are the simple days I'll cherish. Thank you, God, for everything. I'm so, so blessed.

July 9, 2020. Well, here we are. I'm happy that the day is finally here. Festivities start at 4 p.m. I can't believe Matt isn't here for his own birthday party. Happy birthday Matthew, I love you. I'll always love you. I hope to honor you and to make you proud today. After today, we'll really be able to pick up the pieces *and "move along," as you used to say. We'll start anew; our next chapter begins tomorrow. Happy, happy birthday. I love you always and forever. I read this letter out loud to our guests:*

Dear Matthew,

Happy birthday dear husband! Today you would have turned 50, and I never would have guessed in a million years, I'd be spending this day with all of our close friends and family at our lake house—but without you. Life sure can throw you a curve ball.

It's been 224 days since you've been gone, and it's been difficult, to say the least. It's 224 days since I've talked to my best friend, my partner, and the father of our three amazing children. There was only one day in the past 224 days that I thought, "I wish I'd never met you, Matt Gall." But then I stopped and looked around and saw our beautiful kids, our wonderful family, and all of our friends. I am grateful that I met you. Thank you, and I thank God for the past 20 years of marriage and a beautiful life.

When I met you in Chicago on that snowy evening in 1998, it must have been destiny because you really weren't my type.

You were shorter than all of my previous boyfriends, and I had never dated a face painter. You were proud of dressing up like the Ultimate Badger Warrior, like that was normal or something. You wore a red speedo with that wig—quite the costume, but certainly not my type.

What drew me in was your heart. You loved being a doctor because you loved helping others. Your drive and dedication were very impressive. You went a hundred miles an hour full speed ahead, and I loved that you didn't let anything stop you.

You proposed with a spectacular scavenger hunt through the city of Chicago. That was thoughtful and sweet, even if you couldn't afford it. You "charged it!" and prayed that the charges wouldn't get denied in my presence. It was such a great day...one I'll never forget. Living in Chicago in our twenties was the best. Great restaurants, friends, and concerts. We went mountain biking at Kettle Moraine and took inexpensive trips to Florida and Arizona. We partied hard and worked doubly as hard.

We left Chicago for downtown Minneapolis. And that was great and hard at the same time. Your fellowship program at the University of Minnesota was tough, and we were living in our cozy condo, yet longing for a house and kids.

I really wanted to move back to my hometown, and I'll never forget the look on your face when we were house hunting and you saying, "I've worked *this* hard for *this*?" "Yup, and we've got to tear it down," I said. That put you over the edge, and construction in Eden Prairie began.

It was a dream come true, and I was initially obsessed with the house. I overlooked the fact that this is where we'd raise our children, meet the most amazing friends and neighbors, and lay down roots. The memories from our old home are priceless: the parties, the kids running around, the mancave, the hot tub, the big over-the-top Christmas party, the lawn, the grilling, the holidays, the laughter, the tears, the unexpected unplanned fun in that house. It was a happy house, and for 16 years we loved it.

I know things were never 100 percent easy for you, Matthew. The layers of stress you endured were sometimes too much. And now piecing it all together makes sense.

Sort of. Well, not really. You couldn't see what we all saw—and that was a way out.

The last three months of your life were terrifying for me. God was pulling me in, and I tried desperately to save you. Every single person here tried because we all love you so much.

So, as we stand here on what would have been your 50th birthday, I want to say: I love you and thank you.

Thank you for our first-born son, Grady. He is not only handsome, but wise. He doesn't give himself enough credit, but he is smart. He is going to do amazing things. I know you're proud of him that he's going to University of Wyoming. It's going to be great—better than great.

Thank you for Gavin. Gavin is so much like you, it's scary. What a phenomenal memory this kid has. He is a loyal friend like you were to many. Gavin is funny and smart, and this kid is going places...but you probably already know that.

And then Sophie. Matthew, thank you for Sophie. She's sunshine and happiness and fun. She has your kind heart. We don't know if she'll be a surgeon or a fashion designer, but we all have a hunch she's going to light the world on fire.

Matt, I'm sad and sorry that things turned out this way. I want you to know that I'll always love you. I'll try my best to guide these kiddos with your love in my heart and God by my side. I know we will survive, and we will make you proud. We will keep your memory alive by telling stories, taking care of the lawn, celebrating holidays cherishing our time together—we're going to "get it all in." I know that's what you'd want for us. You'll never really be gone, honey, for you'll live in each of us every day. Thank you, thank you for our beautiful kids, and thank you for providing us with what was and what will continue to be, a fabulous life. Here's to the slow fade, the music may be softer, but will never be turned off.

I think that was the greatest party I've ever thrown. It was truly perfect. After an early morning storm, the humidity broke, the sky parted its clouds, the rain was gone, and we were left with partly cloudy skies and 82°. The party went as I planned: white hydrangeas, white tablecloths, balloons, white, of course. Everyone arrived safely. Almost everyone that mattered to us was there.

After I read my birthday letter to Matt, the kids, Liberty, and I took out our boat. Gavin drove, and when we anchored, I released Matt's ashes. When we finished, Sophie released her one white balloon, and then our guests did the same. It was beautiful watching from the boat, to see all 50 white balloons floating over the sparkling lake—it was quite a spectacular vision. Then, dinner was served. I loved that I hired help as Cynda suggested. Their presence allowed me to concentrate on enjoying the party. Drinks were poured, many, many drinks, and stories were told. It was an incredibly meaningful evening. I know we made Matthew proud and that he was smiling down on us. Grady was so much fun last night. All of the kids were awesome.

Now, I sit here in the backyard with my books, my Bible, and my coffee on the most spectacular day ever. Listening to the loons, looking at the sparkling water, the clear blue sky—how is it that you are so good to me, God? Thank you for this beautiful life. Thank you for my kids, my health, my family, and my friends. This has been one amazing ride, and I'm preparing for the next chapter where I vow to enjoy every moment of it.

Chapter 15
Perspective on Medicine Today

During my years as a doctor's wife, I was able to meet several interesting doctors. When I reached out now, related to this book, asking about the "status of medicine today," they anonymously provided me with their perspective and thoughts. These are personal opinions— and it certainly is food for thought for anyone thinking about becoming a doctor today.

Dr. Number One:

The nation faces a projected shortage of between 37,800 and 124,000 physicians within 12 years—according to "The Complexities of Physician Supply and Demand: Projections from 2019 to 2034," a report released by the Association of American Medical Colleges (AAMC).

When we lose a physician by reduced hours, by burn-out and they quit, or worse-case scenario, they die by suicide, it is devastating to the medical infrastructure because of the finite number of physicians available.

People don't understand that medical school class size is directly tied to funding residency training programs. It is a complex system. We can't have more medical students graduating than US residency programs can absorb. Therefore, we have a fixed number of medical school spots and a fixed number of residency spots, and those residency spots are divided into different subspecialties. So, you can't easily "make up" for it when we lose a doctor. And when we do lose one, it puts additional strain on our existing doctors that remain in the workforce. This causes further unhappiness and dissatisfaction within our physician community. It is a continuous negative feedback loop. Our doctors are already overworked. They are already stressed. They don't have enough time as it is. Yet, the work remains—therefore having fewer doctors is good for absolutely no one. This is a really bad trend that was exasperated by the pandemic.

Surprisingly, most of a resident's salary is funded by the US government. This funding emanated from congressional hearings that occurred during the formation of Medicare in 1965. The government funding of graduate medical education serves a strong public interest. A knowledgeable, trained, experienced, and skilled physician workforce is essential to provide the health care needed for our society. I would argue investing in a physician workforce that largely remains in your country, and takes care of your citizens, is good for America. After training, that doctor set up a practice, pays taxes and adds positively to the GDP.

Ultimately, turnover or physician loss has adverse effects on the people that doctors care for. That's you and me! This can lead to increased wait times and can force many patients to travel exorbitant distances to see necessary specialists. This can also lead to interruption of continuity of care—truly it is not good for anyone and has a serious negative impact on a hospital's bottom line.

Dr. Number Two:

As physicians, we really enjoy what we do. We love our patients. We became physicians to help people. We like figuring out ways to detect and solve medical problems.

Things changed in society when health care organizations entered the system via the different insurance options. This includes both group insurance and private insurance companies. It changed the value and status of a doctor. Physicians no longer owned their practice—and they became employees of large organizations within the health care system.

This has led to some inefficiency. We see people in health care administration (the "suits" as Dr. Matthew Gall would refer to them) who do not understand what it means to be a physician—and they make decisions that are detrimental to the physician and his or her medical practice.

The formula is dysfunctional. One of the main issues is the forced time limit with each patient. We might need more time to discuss their needs and consider different alternatives.

Doctors used to be business men, captain of their own ship. They ran lean-and-mean operations in their own clinics that were designed for their patients—who were the source that affected their bottom line.

Medicine has shifted away from the small business world to now all doctors being employed by a large company where they have to follow the guidelines of the administration. Efficiency has been introduced into medicine, causing some bad business decisions—and certainly putting more pressure on the doctor. "Suits" at the administration level are the enemy of happiness for many in the medical field. Administrative "bloat" has been introduced into the system.

More and more pressure is being placed on the physician to see more patients a day—and to do more imaging and testing—as it all means more dollars for the company. Pressure just gets amplified. Many doctors find today that their salaries/income/earning potential has dropped by a third—and this is while the CEO of the health care company receives a huge bonus.

Doctors have families and expenses, too. Salaries are shrinking, and physicians have a high tax rate. Younger doctors are still paying off high medical school expenses, which today can be up to $300,000-plus in tuition, along with high taxes. The average doctor is just hoping to recoup his medical school expenses in his practice; in fact, by the time that dollar amount is paid off, it will now be equivalent to about $400,000.

Dr. Number Three:

The primary care model should be cash only, where you pay the physician for the care you receive. This has received a high patient-satisfaction rate. Medicine is still a noble and honorable profession. We doctors love our patients, but we detest the structures set up by administrators at some of the companies we work for—and there is dissatisfaction at a much higher rate than the public realizes.

Doctors are tired, worn out, and too beaten down by their "employer's rules"—and they do what they can to get through today. The company realizes that they don't need to pay a physician a $300,000-plus salary, when a physician assistant makes $100,000 annually and can do much of the tasks related to mid-level practice. In fact, some physicians are being phased out by administration.

Doctors want to provide excellent care to you and your loved ones. But all these new aspects of "doing business" puts more pressure on the doctor and takes an emotional toll.

This is a system that is "malevolently cursed," and in order for medicine today to become what it desires to be, *physicians at large need to take back power and control.*

This dysfunction can be corrected, but doctors need to become active in business administration of health care. Better situations = better outcomes = better care. We in medicine have to tell the truth in today's world. There needs to be greater support from medical credentialing boards to invest in physicians' well-being. We shouldn't have to fight the system we work for.

Chapter 16
Our Life after Matthew's Suicide

I had never been touched by suicide before my husband took his own life. I did not know one single person who died by suicide; therefore, I did not think much about it. I was so, so naïve because I thought mental illness only affected those homeless, crazy people that roamed the streets mumbling to themselves. I didn't ever think this sickness could affect my husband, *especially* since he was a physician—and he was so smart. I truly don't think he ever thought he could be affected by mental illness either. As mentioned previously, Matthew once told our son Grady, "Don't use your depression as a crutch." He also said that "suicide is for cowards." I truly don't think that Matthew understood depression before it hit him. Or maybe he did, and he kept it to himself for fear of losing his medical license. Matt had a pretty black-and-white way of thinking—but as I have come to understand now—*there is so much gray.*

In general, I am such an optimistic, happy person with a pretty sweet life—so why would I give suicide much thought? I have to say; some days suicide is the only thing that consumes my thoughts. For me, this has been the hardest part of Matthew's death. Any other way of dying would have been much easier to process. Some old friends were (or possibly still are) mad at him. Our whole world changed the day Matthew died, and it had a ripple effect that spans to thousands of people. Some people blame Matthew for his own death—*the one we grieve is the one we blame because he pulled the trigger*. But I've always said…it wasn't him. I repeat this over and over—he wasn't himself. He got sick. Before Matthew died, I was clueless about suicide, as it had always seemed like a selfish act to me. But now I've come to learn that the victim often actually feels as though he or she is a burden. It breaks my heart that Matthew felt like a burden and that he thought the world would be better off without him. Looking back, I cannot believe I was so clueless and so judgmental. Ick, that is not the person who I am today, that's for sure.

After long hours talking with my therapist, researching, and reading about suicide, I have now come to understand that depression is a disease like cancer, and we need to treat it as such. Matthew's brain was attacked, so in his mind, he believed taking his own life was the only way to end the pain.

Doctors need to be able to seek help. If we don't help our doctors stay healthy, who will help us when we get sick?

Chapter 17

What Has Helped Me the Most Through This Journey?

My faith in God—and being grateful
I remember my pastor calling me from Minnesota a few days after Matthew died. He told me that Mathew was *not* in hell, and that he was indeed in heaven. That the fact that Matthew had *committed* a "mortal sin," as the Catholic Church used to refer to, or that Matthew was in "hell," was old theology. Phew…that was a major relief. This had been weighing heavily on my mind, so I was glad that my pastor brought it up. I was also very confused because Matthew had a deep faith. He was a Christian and believed in and loved God. Matthew and I prayed together and often. He even prayed with some of his patients. His own grandfather was a pastor. My pastor's words were comforting to me. They gave me peace knowing that my husband was safe at home in the arms of our Lord. I don't believe that what happened to

Matthew was God's doing or God's will. I believe God gives us free will, and that is why something like this can happen. God is love, and I know God loved Matthew. For me, God was the only one that could bring comfort to this seemingly overwhelming and unbelievable situation.

We must take the word "committed" out of our vocabulary when referring to suicide. It's correct to say "died by suicide." Committed makes it sounds like a crime. Matthew had no more control over his illness than anyone else with a terminal disease.

I believe that there are no coincidences. I believe only in God. I've turned my life over to Him. When a loved one dies by suicide, you instantly become a detective—always searching for clues or answers. Only God has all of the answers. We do not; therefore, we must be okay with sitting in the unknown.

Going to church saved me while Matthew was suffering from his depression, and my Bible study gave me insight to many Christian teachings. My church in North Carolina continues to be a place where I can find comfort and peace. I tell my kids that the church is made up of people—so *find good people*. I do not consider myself religious, but maybe I am. The word "religious" conjures up rules for me, and let's say that I haven't always been the best rule follower. I swear a lot. I am a Christian. I am spiritual. My suggestion is that you find your higher power, whatever that may be.

I wake up early every morning around four or five and make some coffee. I read my morning prayers and devotionals. I read a few scriptures. I pray. I meditate and set my intentions for the day. They usually start out something like this: Thank you God for breath in my lungs, and thank you for my healthy children. It's a new day, and I am going to try and be happy today. You need to be grateful, and my "thankful" list scattered throughout my journals helped me to focus on the positive.

I used to be a news junkie, but I had to turn off the news. As of today, I can honestly say I don't watch the news. I needed initial information regarding the coronavirus, but when we got back to Minnesota, I turned if off completely. I wouldn't say that I am completely clueless when it comes to world events, but I do not watch the news in entirety at all. I can't take hearing about school shootings or war. I can't take on any more unhappiness or fear. The saying *ignorance is bliss* really rings true with me.

As my pastor in North Carolina always says, "It's a blessing to be a blessing." So I try to be that day after day.

I used to wake up and spend my morning balancing my checkbook or checking the stock market, watching the news, making lists, and planning my already overly planned day. Now I wake up and focus on what is important: God. My children. Being grateful. My journals are my personal thoughts and letters to God. I seal my words with the universe when I write. And I am able to work out my issues by putting pen to paper.

My family and friends

Obviously, it was extremely important to surround myself with people that loved me and loved Matthew. My family has been amazing. My brother Bo showed up for me in North Carolina a mere 12 hours after Matt died, on Thanksgiving Day. We have rallied together, and we talk about Matt. We say his name. We tell stories and laugh. We cry and choke up a lot, too.

Thanksgiving will never ever be the same for our family. It used to be my favorite holiday, with no pressure to buy the perfect gift. Just show up and eat. Oh, how Matthew loved to eat. I have had to put my kids first. I can't take on everyone else's grief, nor is it my responsibility to do so. I know my parents love me like crazy, but initially I had to put distance between us. It was hard for me to be around them because I know how much they love me and how hard it was for them to see me devastated. They also miss my husband, as he was like a son to them, which is why I say: I can't imagine ever having to watch Grady, Gavin, or Sophie suffer as I have by losing a spouse. It's hard enough watching them grieve their father now. I wish I could have articulated this better to my parents early on, but I did later. I subconsciously was trying to protect them—and frankly, protect myself. It's difficult dealing with my own grief, let alone dealing with everyone else's. I hate watching my family cry. Matt was larger than life, and he left a huge gaping hole in all of our lives.

My real true friends have been utterly phenomenal, my close childhood girlfriends in particular. We go way back, so I can trust them and count on them always and for anything. I do have one friend from the group, Megan, who I've known since second grade. To this day she still somehow manages to drop everything for me when I call. She listens to me bawl, she helps me work through my feelings, which can be all over the board, and she is there to laugh with me, too. She is my voice of reason, and my rock. I can trust her for sound advice. I don't know how she does it, especially considering the fact that we talk at least three times a day. I tell everyone that they should be so lucky as to have a "Megan" in their lives. She's been my person.

My childhood girlfriends showed up in North Carolina the day after Thanksgiving. They did everything for me. They swooped in, made arrangements, helped sort, organize, and manage my shattered life immediately following Matt's death. They are my heart and soul. I'll never be able to repay them for everything they did for me.

And then, there are my North Carolina girlfriends, who stood by me without hardly even knowing me. Here I was, some random woman from Minnesota that they had known for only three months. Jennifer and her son and another friend of Gavin's actually flew to Minnesota for Matthew's funeral. It was expensive, and this gesture touched my family beyond belief. These seven special ladies took care of me when we returned back to North Carolina after Matthew's funeral. They took me out for Valentine's Day. They surrounded me with love. They carried me; they still do. And yes, I know that the number seven has significant meaning, too. These girls are good people—and I knew that from the moment I met them. I am so lucky and smile when I think about each and every one of them.

Sadly, a few important people once in our lives are not anymore. You learn that *suicide brings about judgment and speculation from others.* This was another aspect surrounding Matthew's death that I didn't expect. I lost people who I thought were my friends. I'll never understand how someone can turn on a friend who is suffering. Unfortunately, I know what the term "silence is deafening" now means. It's been horrible, to say the least.

If people are not happy and rooting for you, say goodbye. Early on, certain friends stopped including me—and believe me, I am not one to get caught up in not being invited to everything. I knew things would eventually change, but to have it happen so early hurt immensely. I felt that their actions were intentional. I had to block people on social media because I didn't want to see what I was missing out on. Matthew and I had created a large social network, and to see our friends carrying on without us really stung. Knowing things would change eventually was hard enough, but then to hear that they were talking about me behind my back felt malicious.

I now know that suicide makes you more sensitive, too. You can't help but feel the stares and the chatter going on behind your back. *"Rejoice with those who rejoice; mourn with those who mourn."* – Romans 12: 15

Initially, I really didn't want to move back to Minneapolis from North Carolina. I knew people would look at me differently. And they did. I'll never forget the afternoon I walked into our local grocery store, and a neighbor who I hadn't seen since Matthew's death looked at me square in the eyes, then quickly looked away. I felt awful, ashamed, and embarrassed. This person wasn't a close friend, but she knew what happened. She is a nice lady so maybe she didn't know what to say or how to react, but by her turning away without saying *anything really* hurt me.

While there are never perfect words to soothe a weeping soul, a simple hug, smile or, "Betsy, I don't know what to say," would have been so much better than looking the other way.

The most pain doesn't come from well-meaning words—*it comes from silence.*

My suggestion is this, simply surround yourself with true friends. Friends that show up. Friends that talk to you, friends that run toward you, not away from you. Forgiving the people that have hurt you along your journey — and unfortunately there will be those people—you need to eventually do that and let it go. I've spent thousands of hours and thousands of dollars in therapy trying to figure out why. It takes time to forgive, but I have. I can only chalk it up to *people just don't understand. We all miss Matthew.*

My Suicide Support Group

Upon moving back to Minnesota, I knew I needed to find a group that understood what I was going through. I actually stumbled upon my support group while searching online for grief support for Sophie. I remember the first meeting like it was yesterday. It was held at a local church instead of the grief center because of Covid. When I arrived, I just sat in my car. I stared out the window thinking to myself: *I'd rather be anywhere else on the planet than here.* I was feeling paralyzed with fear and had no idea what to expect. *Betsy Gall is at a suicide support group,* I thought to myself. *This can't be real.*

But I did get out of the car, and I put one foot in front of the other until I got to the meeting. "Big Widow," our group leader, was the first to greet me with a warm smile and a big hug. Looking back, I am so happy that I went to that meeting, and I continue to go even some days when I don't feel like it. Someone else may need me; I may be the person to help a fellow widow. So I show up, and we "get our grief on," as my special friends and I like to jokingly say.

I thank God for these women. We meet once a month, and it's one of my most important gatherings. Every one of us has a different story, yet our chapters are woven together with many similarities. *Unfortunately, our group continues to grow.* I'll never forget the darling member that said, "My life is going to be better than it was before." I was shocked by her fearless statement. *Can we say things like this?* I thought to myself. It was such a bold statement about hope for a fantastic future. Well guess what? Yes! You can say that. I say this now without regret because it's true. I've been to hell and back, and I am going to have a life that is better than before. This doesn't mean that I love my husband any less.

I said the other night at our meeting, "Love wasn't enough to keep our husbands alive. If it was, none of us would be sitting here tonight. You can't *love* the cancer out of someone. Mental illness is a sickness, and it needs to be treated as such." It's so simple and true, but takes so long for that fact to sink in.

Losing a spouse to suicide is the absolute worst. If your spouse dies of an illness or a car accident, you can blame that. Even murder—you have another person to blame. But with suicide, you blame the one you loved, the one you are grieving. It's confusing and complicated. There are too many emotions that cannot be explained unless you've been through it. Getting into a widow's suicide support group was essential. They get me. There is no judgment, only love and understanding. We discuss everything; no topic is off the table. Believe me, you'll need your support people.

Betsy's Monthly Suicide Support Group

Susan, (aka Big Widow) facilitator of my suicide support group, shares about her group's sense of community. She has led this group through Brighter Days Family Grief Center in Eden Prairie, Minnesota, for almost seven years. Susan also facilitates another grief group through an organization called Widow Might. And sadly, we all speak the same language.

◆ ◆ ◆

Suicide death is complex, as it has extra layers. It is considered "traumatic loss." Those who struggle set their goals so high for themselves related to work or other things—and then something goes wrong.

This group is a sanctuary for those left behind by suicide. It's important to reach out to a group or get into therapy—don't try to go it alone because it can be very traumatic to suffer in silence. Everyone needs to be surrounded by a "community" where they can connect, because this kind of death is different and more complicated. There's pressure and judgment from society about suicide. Many issues led up to these types of deaths.

The most important messages to the women in our group are:

- You should have no shame in having a loved one die by suicide. It's not your fault.
- You are not alone.
- You will continue to go through grief, working through your shock, shame, and the feeling of being abandoned.
- The question "Why?" becomes an immediate—and also lingering question. And you may never find the answer.
- In fact, you will find yourself questioning most areas in your new life. You wonder why you didn't know and what you could have done to help.
- As with all grief, it's okay to not deal with everything right now.
- There will never be any judgment in our group.
- Your loss might feel "messy."
- It is important to talk about specific things, so you begin to feel, "I can handle this."
- Suicide still has a strong social stigma to it.

- In the future, you will learn to walk alongside your grief.
- It's okay to be vulnerable.
- Other members will understand, offer suggestions, walk and talk with you, and also lend a hand.

Other members in our group tell their stories because they understand what you are going through—and that eventually you will get through it. The story of every one of almost 20 women matters, and we often hear, "I used to feel that way, too." We found that sharing helps others in their healing. We have many "ah-ha" moments in the group, like "My husband was like that, too"—which brings a sense of comfort.

Those whose loved one died by suicide are left with more than grief—we have many unanswered questions. Usually with suicide, the police are involved (and sometimes, the media), which brings forth questions from others. Grief is grief, but loss by suicide is a whole lot more complicated. You cannot prepare yourself for the journey ahead. If you have children, you now have to be the voice of positivity as your family moves into the future. You also have to be aware your children are more at risk when a family member dies by suicide.

About half of the women in our group had no idea that their husband was depressed, and because many do not leave a note, you try to figure out what would cause him to do something so permanent—and how it happened. Now they belong to a "community" of women who understand and who can relate to exactly what you are going through because there is such a stigma related to mental illness, and especially suicide.

A suicide death has many forms of loss—it adds an extra layer, and those left behind try to answer the "whys." You are dealing with the loss of your loved one and the life you had together. Some questions from family, friends, and even strangers are quite shocking and intrusive. People say inappropriate things—not to be mean, but because they don't realize what they are saying.

When you are being judged by others, some common questions might be:

- Did you have marital problems?
- What was happening in your family?
- Did he have life insurance—and will it pay off because it was suicide?
- Did he have a secret family someplace else?
- Does depression run in the family? (True for less than half in our group.)
- One widow was actually approached by a friend with the statement of, "I thought he loved you."

If they have children, the women tell how much the men had loved their children and their life—and that they were great dads. Women are strong. They become so capable of dealing with everyday life and have personal power. Many women continue with some form of therapy for a long time.

I love to see the women in our group grow, blossom, and eventually move forward to embrace life again. At early meetings for a new widow, there are lots of tears every time she speaks. I eventually see her become empowered, and then she ends up helping others. Our group is helpful so these women *don't feel so alone*. Sometimes their sense of humor is very funny—it's called a widow's humor. We have widows from late-30s to mid-60s. It's good to share because you get input from different ages.

Did these men try suicide before their fatal try? Of our group, it's true for about 20 percent. Sadly, mental illness or addiction takes over and is in charge when he ends his life.

Finally, it is appreciated by the family who lost a loved one by suicide if you share stories and say his name. I just received a touching card from a friend on the anniversary of my husband's death—his "Angel-versary." It said, "In Memory…" and they wrote a note and made a donation to suicide prevention in his name. I was very moved that they were thinking of me more than a decade later.

To find a group in your city/area for those left behind, contact the national organization or its local chapter:

- National Alliance on Mental Illness (NAMI) – www.NAMI.org
- American Foundation for Suicide (AFSC) Prevention – www.AFSP.org

◆ ◆ ◆

Getting professional help has been essential

I love my girlfriends, but they are not equipped to handle something as serious as suicide. They are not therapists. We were all very confused early on. I urge you to seek professional help. My kids and I went to family therapy together a few times, then we all saw (and still do see) individual therapists. It's important to remember that *we all grieve differently*. I still see my trusted psychotherapist every single week. She is a guide who helps me sort through feelings and helps me *to not be so hard on myself*. This has been tough because when you lose someone you love to suicide, it inevitably brings along guilt.

Emotions of Suicide:

There are many mixed emotions when it comes to suicide. The act itself may seem like an assault on or rejection of those of us left behind. Why wasn't I enough? Why weren't our kids enough? These are often feelings that roll through our minds. And then there are the "what ifs." What if I hadn't found that recruiter? What if we'd never moved to North Carolina? These questions we ask may be extreme and self-punishing—unrealistically condemning the survivor for failing to predict the death or to intervene effectively or on time.

Experts tell us that in such circumstances, survivors *tend to greatly overestimate their own contributing role—and their ability to affect the outcome.*

The feelings of anger, rejection, and abandonment that occur after many deaths are especially intense and difficult to navigate after a suicide occurs.

Dealing with the Shame, Betrayal, and Trauma of Suicide

– Shame

If you look up the word *shame* in the dictionary, it states: a painful feeling of humiliation or distress caused by the consciousness of wrong or foolish behavior. It is a condition that condemns somebody for being dishonorable or disgraceful.

One of the first things that runs through your mind when a loved one dies by suicide is: *What will people think?* I remember being worried about my neighbors. We were new to the neighborhood, and they didn't really know us. What would they think about my late husband or my family? Matthew truly was loved by so many; would people think it was *my* fault? What would his patients think? He had dedicated his entire life to saving lives. Think about that for a moment. What would our friends think? I did let his close friends know early on that he was suffering; they knew it, yet there was nothing they could do or say to make Matthew seek help. Some came to visit him in North Carolina, and the "five guys" as I refer to them, knew Matt was very sick. He was simply not himself. And I wonder…if they blame me for the move to North Carolina, therefore they must blame me for his death.

I've worked really hard on this section because not only am I dealing with guilt, anger, regret, and confusion, but I am overwhelmed with sadness. You don't have to worry about these issues if someone dies in a car accident. It's just sad. My husband, the father of my children, is dead—and not coming back. I still have a hard time wrapping my brain around this. I've now joined a secret club: one that nobody wants to be a member of. I hate it.

We need to deny shame when it comes to our feelings regarding suicide. We need to let go of the feeling— because we did not cause our loved one's mental illness. We could not control the outcome any more than someone trying to love a terminal disease out of someone.

– Betrayal

Matthew was my best friend, and we talked about everything. Until the day he took his own life. We didn't discuss this: how we were going to die. He and his friends may have spent a lot of guy time together and confided in each other, but Matthew came home and told me *everything*. He couldn't help himself; he was almost childlike in a way as he was unable to keep a secret. We bickered, yes, but at the end of the day, I had his back and he had mine. We were typically united. Our marriage was not perfect; I don't think perfect marriages exist. I remember standing in my bedroom a few days before Matt died, holding a picture of our three young kids fishing off our dock. I held the picture up and said, "Matt, this is going to be our grandkids one day." He said, "I hope so." I had never seen him so defeated; it was like he'd already given up. I pleaded with him repeatedly to please listen to me and get help. He didn't, and I felt betrayed by him for a long time. But now I realize that he was super sick. Matt didn't have control over his mental illness any more than his patients had control over their cancer.

I've had to let these feeling go, too. I have been able to do so only through prayer and therapy. It takes a lot of work to process all of these feelings. It's not fun, and it's not easy.

– Trauma

Trauma is an emotional response to a terrible event. Immediately after the event, shock and denial are typical. Longer-term reactions can include unpredictable emotions, flashbacks, strained relationships, and even physical symptoms. I did a couple of sessions of EMDR therapy. Eye movement desensitization and reprocessing is a form of psychotherapy developed to alleviate the distress associated with traumatic memories such as PTSD. I personally did not find the therapy useful, but I know others who swear by it. Even though I didn't see Matthew pull the trigger or see his body after he died, I still am traumatized. I choose to work through these feelings with my therapist.

Every person is on a different journey in this life. The following is how I coped with our tragic loss.

As you've read, Matthew's suicide made me question every single decision I'd ever made in my entire life. This included decisions ranging from saying yes to marrying him, to where we sent our kids to school, to money we'd spent, to even building our house. The "what ifs," blame, and shame were endless.

Every thought I had was negative, and I didn't stop beating myself up. It was only with the help of my trusted therapist that I was able to let that go. It's taken over two and a half years, but I now understand that these decisions didn't cause Matthew's mental illness—*and that I alone didn't have the power to stop his sickness.* I didn't cause it. I couldn't control it nor could I cure it.

Thoughts from My Therapist

The most important thing to do after losing someone to suicide is to seek professional help. Betsy's story is so valuable—and the real message is getting help from professionals when you have mental health needs. Allowing a mental health issue to go untreated increases the risk of your health deteriorating. Removing the stigma and shame about mental illness requires all of us to value and embrace our own mental wellness.

Trying to make sense of a tragic loss by yourself can be confusing and limiting. *Denying the need for working with mental health professionals feeds the idea that we should be able to manage our mental wellness alone.* This in turn makes us falsely believe we are weak if we can't.

In reality, it takes more courage and strength to reach out for help—even when you are afraid you will lose everything if you do—because losing their medical license is a possibility for some medical professionals.

Seeking professional help to understand your own mix of emotions, what was happening for your loved one, and knowing that there is treatment for mental illness, is extremely important. People really do get better. Getting help for yourself is the best way to honor your loved one and respect your own personal journey with grief and healing.

Exercise and Eating Right

Exercise was an easy one for me because I have always loved to work out. It was important to me to keep a routine and move my body. Sweating and spending an hour or two every morning outside or in the gym is therapeutic. I find the time by myself to be important. I put on inspirational music and move my body. I run, I do the stair-stepper machine, and I go to classes. I take sculpt, Pilates, barre, yoga, GTX, shred, and strength classes. You name it, if there is a class, I go. It doesn't matter what you do—but it is important that you do something.

A simple suggestion comes from the book *Healing After Loss* by Martha Hickman. It is daily meditations for working through grief. Hickman reminds us exercise, especially walking, is an empowering action because it takes you somewhere—and you are moving away from sadness and depression. When you are "stuck" on something, she says *get out and walk!*

I take a lot of walks, and it truly helps you push the reset button when you need it.

My weight has always been a struggle for me. I've lost roughly twenty pounds because of grief and getting coronavirus. I am just so much more attuned with my body now, so keeping the weight off hasn't been difficult for me at all. I try and listen to what my body needs in order to make good choices. While I'll always have an affinity for jelly beans, I know that when I look better, I feel better.

I really had to watch myself with the drinking. It's so easy to just keep pouring the wine, *because numbing your feelings and masking the pain feels good.* But I knew that waking up hungover wasn't going to help me in the long run. It wasn't good for me or my kids. If I am going to be completely honest, my drinking was going down the wrong path—and that path was beginning to become a slippery slope. I could have easily slid right into that bottle and stayed there a while. I did get a wake-up call from a very close friend. My drinking was drudging up an ugliness that isn't who I really am. Now I try and keep the drinking to a minimum. I'm happy to report that I have been quite successful in this arena.

Adding yoga and meditation has been life-changing

Yoga helps me immensely. I was never anxious before Matthew got sick. Anxiety is an ugly, uncomfortable feeling, but yoga helps alleviate those unpleasant feelings for me. You can connect your body and mind through movement and breath control. Yoga has been known to lower stress and bring down blood pressure. I find the practice very calming, which is something I need more of in my life. I had no idea what I was doing when I began taking yoga classes. Luckily for me, my instructor was kind, patient, and helpful. A good yoga instructor shows authenticity in their personality; they have energy and true passion for their teachings.

I have read several books on meditation and positive thinking. It's been easier for me to listen to meditations on podcasts or YouTube when I am trying to fall asleep at night. Breathing deeply, and simply pausing, has helped me to be still and to take in God's glory. I'm not going to lie; meditation has been more difficult for me because I'm not used to being quiet. I've filled my life up with construction projects and busyness so that I wouldn't have a moment to think about the depth of my pain. But being still is important. You need stillness in order to connect with your intuitiveness and to be able to listen to your gut.

Trying new things and putting myself out there

You need to wake up every day and put on the coffee. You need to make your bed, put on your makeup, and put one foot in front of the other. While it'd be easy to stay in bed with the covers over your head, it just wasn't an option for me with three teenagers to raise. It's also not in my DNA. I am a go-getter and have always believed that you need to live boldly and without regret.

I know people have judged me for the way I grieve, but *you need to stop caring about what others think and do it your way.* There are no rules when it comes to grief. It is not a linear process that you can go through, checking off boxes. Believe me, I tried that, and it doesn't work that way. It is raw and terrifying and sneaks up on you when you least expect it.

When we first moved to North Carolina, I vowed to say "yes" to everything. I was asked, "Do you want to learn to go wake boarding?" I said yes. My kids asked, "Mom, do you want to go water skiing today?" I said yes—even though I secretly didn't want to. "Betsy, will you speak to our group about your loss?" Gulp. I chose to say yes even though it was challenging, but I knew our story would help others. I say yes because I don't want to have any regrets. Saying yes...it's the least I can do. Just say yes, if you can, and you'll be pleased that you did.

I know it is a cliché, but life is so short you truly need to live it and love it while you can. Life can change in an instant; in my life there will always be the "before" the suicide and the "after."

I met a wonderful guy about a year after Matthew passed away. It's scary dating after having been married for twenty years. I felt damaged and couldn't even wrap my head around that fact that someone would even want to date me—someone like me with such heavy baggage.

This person came into my life when I desperately needed hope. Ironically, this man just happened to speak with Matthew on his last day at The Group. This amazing person is also a physician, a plastic surgeon, and he and Matthew shared a mutual patient that they discussed that day. Over our 14 months together, I was reminded once again about the stresses that *all* of our doctors are facing.

I was so sick of people looking at me with pity in their eyes. I thought having a boyfriend would make that stop. We fell in love with each other quickly; I think both of us were tired of feeling sad. But at the end of the day, it just wasn't right. He had his own issues to deal with stemming from his painful divorce. Although the relationship didn't work out, I am so happy that I said yes to that first date. I learned so much about myself: the good, the bad, and the ugly. Relationships are hard work. I know people judged me for dating what felt "too soon" in their eyes, but I needed that special guy at that time in my life.

This ex-boyfriend of mine, we've worked hard at staying friends, too. It hasn't been easy. My kids said it couldn't be done, but I said, "I'm fifty-two years old, and I get to do things my way." The break up was difficult, and I didn't want it to happen because I had heard that breaking up after the loss of a spouse is like going through the death all over again. Dr. Jennifer Ashton is the one who actually told me that. Dr. Ashton of *Good Morning America* and I have become friends since she received my letter. Jen was right; the break-up was painful. I can completely attest to that. While it obviously wasn't as traumatic as Matt's death, I had a hard time letting go, not only because my ex is a fantastic human being, but because I've already lost so many people that I've loved. His nickname for *me* was Hope, but he brought me hope when I needed it most. We brought each other hope, and nobody should ever fault us for that. If I am being completely honest about it, I actually manifested him, but that's a story for a different book. I often thought to myself that I wouldn't write this book until I knew it would have a happy ending. So maybe my next book will be about manifesting true love because I am pretty confident as I write this that the next chapter of my life is going to be fantastic. There is a happy ending in my future.

I learned early on in my life that you never move on. And it's true that I'll never move "on" from losing Matthew, or any person I've loved for that matter, but I will move forward. You have to.

I realized that it's important to set realistic intentions every day. Early on, I was trying to force happiness, but it's just not possible after a trauma of this magnitude occurs. Lately, I've tried to state: *I have no idea what will happen today, but I intend to go with the flow — to make it the best day possible.* I also don't feel guilty about doing nice things for myself, like buying myself flowers or getting a massage. Suicide is terrible and you need to give yourself some grace

Chapter 18
Today We Are Good

It's been roughly two and a half years since Matthew passed away. I'm sitting at our lovely lake house, listening to the loons calling across the lake, and the sun is shining. God is good. The kids are all doing incredibly well. Grady has nicknamed this season of our life as "The Summer of Healing." And it has been. Yes, we have difficult days, but they are not quite as frequent. We talk about Matthew a lot. We remember him and tell funny stories about him. Gavin and Grady do great impersonations of their dad. They make us laugh. I still feel like I am watching a movie about someone else's life—and that this isn't really *my* life. I wonder if that feeling will ever go away?

Matthew was such a happy guy, so the fact that he took his own life will always remain somewhat of a mystery. I know that he loved me and the kids more than anything. Therefore, I can't imagine the *amount of pain he must have been in*. It will always make me sad to think of that. But I've learned that I must continue to lean on God because He has all of the answers, and I do not. I never will.

We've had to let go of doing the lawn just perfectly. Actually, it looks like shit; we can't keep up and don't know how Matthew had it looking so beautiful all of the time. We are planning to head back to North Carolina in late August. I can't believe this even as I write it. Gavin was the one who initially wanted to move back home to Minnesota. He wanted his old life back. He wanted me to buy our old house back, and he wanted to play football at his old high school. Of all three children, Gavin is most like my late husband. While I compromised and was happy to move back to Minnesota for two years, we all realized that "going back" isn't necessarily easy. I am glad we did it, and I do believe that everything happens for a reason.

Late last summer, Gavin herniated his disc, so as it turned out, he couldn't even play football. Thank you, God; I don't ever want my kids to get a concussion. Matthew had at least nine of them over the course of his life, caused from injury while playing sports like rugby and football. We decided as a family to take the plunge and move back to North Carolina. While some people may think we are insane, we have our reasons for moving back. I was lucky enough to be able to keep my home there. I am able to keep my residence in Minnesota, too. We plan on splitting our time between the two states.

Grady is transferring to Colorado State University in the fall, and I am beyond proud of that kid. He has not had an easy life, but he has persevered. My heart bursts with pride when I think about him and all that he has overcome.

Grady's Words...

It's been over two years since I lost my dad. Life is weird and nothing feels the same. I wake up not knowing what to expect—whether or not his memory will even cross my mind.

The days he is on my mind are the hardest. There are so many things I wished I had asked him, so many life skills I never was taught, and most importantly so many things I wish I had done differently. I sometimes see him in my dreams as if things were back to normal, and for a brief moment, I am at peace.

But the reality of the matter is that my dad is gone, and there is nothing that will bring him back. It hurts me because I was never able to tell him how sorry I am...for everything.

My dad always put pressure on me to be the best. Being the oldest son usually comes with that type of pressure. But I was nothing like him—nowhere near as smart or charismatic as he was. I tried so hard to be the son he could be proud of, but I feel as though I failed.

I wish I had more time to prove myself to him. My early teenage years were tough—we did nothing but argue. But things were finally starting to look up for our relationship when we moved to North Carolina. But as you read, things fell apart quickly. I feel like if I had even just one more day with him, he'd still be alive. One more day to show him that I got accepted into college. One more day to show him that out of everybody in the house, I understand his pain, and that I feel for him.

If I had just sat him down and opened up to him about my own battles with depression and suicidal thoughts, maybe he'd realize that he was not alone in this. It never crossed my mind because as men we don't share feelings with each other. Plus, my dad never showed an ounce of sadness in him. He was passionate about everything he did and always made sure everybody was having fun.

Out of all the people in the world, I never expected my own father to take his life. It's still shocking to this day. No matter what, always make sure to check up on the people you love. You never know what someone is going through behind closed doors.

Gavin's Words

It's Father's Day 2022. I am currently at our lake house with five friends. I woke up before everyone, and I'm about to get ready to go mountain biking with my friends, Carter and Ryan. I'm certain that if my dad was alive, we would be getting ready to mountain bike with us.

Unfortunately, that isn't the case. Today, over two-plus years later, it is still hard to believe that I lost my dad to suicide, and I am still greatly affected by the loss of him. My dad's death has robbed me of so many things I should have experienced, had he been with us. These are experiences that span from attending my graduations and future wedding—to going out on the boat or washing the car together.

Now at age 17, even with everything that's happened, I believe *there's a silver lining*. Over the years, my father has shaped me into the person I am today. The conception of him seeing my progress and development over the years inspires me to do better at everything I do, like my education and my health. Because of my father, I know how to live every experience to the fullest and do as he said, by "Getting it all in."

With those euphoric years of my childhood and early teenage years, I try to avoid wishing how good things could be—and I try to remember how lucky I actually am. I have a healthy relationship with everyone in my family. I have good friends. I live in a financially stable household. Many people would love to be in my situation, so complaining and looking at the glass half-empty never helps.

Two and a half years later, I've learned to better myself. *Using my dad as inspiration to do good, rather than a reason to fail, has helped me with my own mental health.*

Sophie's Words

As I write this mid-June 2022, it's been 938 days without my dad. At first, I blinded myself from the truth. I didn't face the fact that my dad was actually gone. I had my good days and my bad days. I would only ever cry when I was alone.

I couldn't see a therapist because of the coronavirus, and online Zoom calls were not the way to go for me. I distracted myself by keeping busy. I struggled with the guilt of thinking I could've done more—that somehow, I could have saved my dad.

Now I am seeing an amazing therapist. I've learned that everything happens for a reason—that this is part of my life and has helped me become who I am today. I couldn't change what Dad's depressed brain had already made up. I cannot control anyone else's mind but mine. I know he is better now that he isn't in pain.

I feel like it's still hard remembering that he's not here anymore. It's hard thinking about all the things he will miss out on, and how it affects me. We never went to a father/daughter dance like he always wanted to. Who is going to take care of my stupid ex-boy-friends? (Thankfully, I have two older brothers.) Who is going to walk me down the aisle at my wedding?

My world has been changed, in a way I never expected. It brought my family closer together. It allowed me to make new friends in different states because of the move. It allows me to have the opportunity to help others who have gone through what I have.

I am currently traveling in Europe with some friends on a World War II trip organized through my high school. I was nervous about coming because some of the girls' fathers are on this trip. I really miss having mine with me.

I am thankful for my family and everyone who has stuck by me during our journey through grief.

◆ ◆ ◆

Betsy recaps their life today

Grady will be a sophomore transfer student at Colorado State University in a few weeks, and he spent this past summer healing. He is still figuring out what he wants to major in, but it doesn't matter because he has a good soul, and I know he will do great things. Gavin has worked his butt off to achieve high grades and a good ACT score because he wants to apply to some excellent colleges next year. He plans to go into finance, and I have no doubt he will conquer his dreams. Miss Sophie just finished her sophomore year in high school. She is our sunshine. She is one of the most positive people I have ever met. She is compassionate and caring. All of my kids are. This tragedy has brought us closer together; we know how important family is. Family is everything.

When death steals one of your own, you can't help but become more compassionate and empathetic

As for me, my real estate business has been booming, and I am grateful to have work that I thoroughly enjoy and am passionate about. I love being a real estate agent, an investor, a landlord, and a habitual remodeler. I believe our homes are the backdrops of our lives, so I take pride in making those spaces beautiful. Helping people find their home is truly a gift for me.

That being said, I have been invited to speak all over the nation regarding physician suicide. Unfortunately, we have a crisis on our hands—and we need *our doctors to be healthy*. If my voice can add to the conversation, and hopefully shed some light on what I believe to be a "secret" crisis within our medical community, I feel a duty to speak out. I say it all the time: If this could happen to Matthew Gall, it could happen to anyone.

I keep putting one foot in front of the other. My kids are my everything, I've spent the last few months trying to be more present for them. I know a time will come when they will be out of the nest. I can hardly think about that, so I try and savor every moment we have together. I know that I will find true love again someday. I'm a "people" person—I thrive on being around people, and for me, being in a committed relationship is important. Deep down, I am still that 26-year-old girl that believes everything is better when you are in love. I do work on trying to be a better version of myself daily. I've done a lot of self-reflection, and I know I've made mistakes along the way, but I have learned from them, and honestly, I am doing the best job that I can. I wish I could say that I am happy every day. I am not; a chunk of my heart will always be missing. I live for moments now. I try and soak up all of the time I have with my children, my family, and my friends. It's the beautiful moments that we will look back on in our lives with those we love that we should savor most. I am positive that with God's love and grace I will find the peace, joy, happiness, and love that my heart desires. Actually, I already have.

Chapter 19

A Crisis Situation

Physician suicide rate is 2x that of general population.[8]

300-400 have estimated to die by suicide every year.[9]

On average, one a physician dies by suicide each day.[10]

55 percent of physicians know a physician who has considered or attempted or died by suicide.[11]

---

[8] https://www.webmd.com/mental-health/news/20180508/doctors-suicide-rate-highest-of-any-profession

[9] 10 Facts About Physician Suicide and Mental Health. American Foundation for Suicide Prevention. https://www.acgme.org/Portals/0/PDFs/ten%20facts%20about%20physician%20suicide.pdf

[10] 10 Facts About Physician Suicide and Mental Health. American Foundation for Suicide Prevention. https://www.acgme.org/Portals/0/PDFs/ten%20facts%20 about%20physician%20suicide.pdf

[11]https://physiciansfoundation.org/physician-and-patient-surveys/the-physicians-foundation-2021-physician-survey/

I really wish that I didn't have to write a book on physician suicide. Sadly, I feel as though it is my mission to speak openly and candidly about a subject that isn't widely talked about. I feel that most doctors are aware that they fall into a vulnerable category—but the subject matter isn't discussed openly. Burnout seems to be a buzz word, but what is being done to change the system?

I am dedicated to doing everything that I can to fight for change, to honor my late husband's legacy, and to ensure that no other family has to go through the same experience.

◆ ◆ ◆

A New Law Aims to Address the Mental Health Among Healthcare Workers—But Barriers to Care Persist

The article's title in *Fortune, Inc.* says it all, as it was written by relatives of a female physician who died by suicide. Both Jennifer Breen Feist and J. Corey Feist, MBA, are attorneys. Corey is a health care executive with over 20 years of experience. I have talked to both Corey and Jennifer directly, and they are the real deal. They are making a difference, and I am dedicated to their cause.

Together they cofounded the *Dr. Lorna Breen Foundation*. In March 2022, President Biden signed the Dr. Lorna

Breen Healthcare Provider Protection Act (HR 1667)—"a first-of-its-kind legislation that aims to reduce and prevent suicide, burnout, and mental and behavioral conditions in healthcare professions."

The Feist story: In April 2020, Dr. Lorna Breen, a New York City emergency room physician, died by suicide. She had been working on the frontline of the first wave of Covid and had been constantly treating a deluge of patients.

Dr. Breen had no history of mental illness, but she had told her sister, Jennifer, that she had been overwhelmed by the vast number of patients—plus the fact that they were understaffed and under-resourced. Yes, this is true across the country, not just New York City.

Dr. Breen was aware of burnout issues—but when she needed help, she didn't receive it. As she told her family, she thought she would be risking losing her medical license—or be ostracized by other medical professionals if she received treatment. Her lack of mental health therapy caused another preventable tragedy.

The Foundation is helping people see that healthcare professionals seeking mental health services should be viewed as a sign of strength—not weakness.

You can help: For details, contact the Dr. Lorna Breen Foundation. social@drbreenheroes.org

The *Dr. Lorna Breen Health Care Provider Protection Act* (HR 1667) aims to reduce and prevent suicide, burnout, and mental and behavioral health conditions among health care professionals. Health care professionals have long experienced high levels of stress and burnout, and COVID-19 has only exacerbated the problem. While helping their patients fight for their lives, many health care professionals are coping with their own trauma of losing patients and colleagues, and fear for their own health and safety. This bill helps promote mental and behavioral health among those working on the frontlines of the pandemic. It also supports suicide and burnout prevention training in health professional training programs and increases awareness and education about suicide and mental health concerns among health care professionals.

Other Excellent Resources

When I read Dr. Michael F. Myers's book, *Why Physicians Die by Suicide: Lessons Learned from Their Families and Others Who Cared*, I was shocked, saddened, and then relieved to see that he put such things into a book.

I went through his book and highlighted the statements that were most relevant to my husband and our life—and things I need to know to help bring this extreme problem to the forefront of doctors and their families.

No family should have someone's death sneak up on them—and sadly, the deceased has now passed his pain onto us, and he's not here to help us with the pain and grief we are left with.

Dr. Myers and I have become fast friends. He is a brilliant psychiatrist and an expert on physician suicide. We've had dinner and we talk on the phone, and he has given me permission to use any and all words of wisdom I find in his book *to help me make a point in my writings and my speeches.*

His Words of Wisdom—verbatim, and at times, slightly paraphrased…

- One million patients a year lose their doctor to suicide.
- Doctors continue to take their own lives at a rate higher than the general population.
- Suicide is the tenth most common cause of death in the United States—a person every 12 minutes.

- The rate is climbing steadily in the last 15–20 years, but has fallen slightly the last two years.
- 1 million people attempt suicide every year—one every 35 seconds.
- 85–90 percent of doctors show some psychiatric illness at the time of their death: depression, alcoholism, other substance abuse, anxiety, or PTSD.
- The person feels hopeless, and self-extinction seems to be the only way out.
- Women doctors are 2–3 times more prone to suicide than average women.
- Suicide is a very taboo subject in public society.
- Doctors can become haunted by failure or even the thought of failure.
- Their life has been focused on perfectionism and self-recrimination—common traits in doctors.
- Doctors thrive on high standards of excellence and precision required by their profession.
- To understand, we need to capture the complexity, the inner conflict, and the irony of self-destruction and despair in the "guardians of our life."
- Many exciting and joyful experiences happen in their daily lives, but so do challenges that deal with the business end of being a doctor, adding many unavoidable stresses:
  - Increased documentation

- Learning about electronic health records (EHRs)
- Keeping up with the latest innovations
- Maintaining competence and licensing
- The demands of patients (and their family members)
- Threats of lawsuits
- Business costs

• Oncologists spend countless hours breaking bad news while trying always to be hopeful, and not grim.

• What makes a doctor's suicide even more tragic and ironic is that often they have been "killed by their work—their lives lost in the line of duty."

• Medical journals and websites are filled with articles on burnout by medical students and doctors— a rate much higher than other professions.

• Membership in this profession is very rigid and exclusive—and they worry that if they seek help, it could be grounds to be thrown out of this club (lose their medical license).

• Shame is often one of the many emotions overwhelming those who make that fateful decision to die by suicide. Do they believe they deserve to die because their inability to practice medicine is bringing dishonor to their profession?

- Some doctors have psychological fears of taking medications for depression, as it acknowledges that their illness is taking over. They worry that they need a "chemical" to get better. Those who rely on their toughness and self-reliance view medications as a "crutch" or "cop out."
- This "dirty little secret" brings fear that if their patients knew…they may lose confidence or go elsewhere.
- Why suicide? Most people who kill themselves are mentally ill—however in medical culture, there is a need to eradicate the stigma and silence associated with suicide—and physicians need to speak out.
- Openness when talking about suicide in the medical field will help us gain respect—not diminish it.
- It is hard to conclude that anything other than mental illness could drive such an unfathomable final act in individuals so fortunate and privileged.
- Because physicians are expected to respect, protect, and preserve life, it is hard to come to terms with the knowledge that a doctor has taken her or his life.
- Therefore, a physician's suicide is too paradoxical a concept for us to contemplate.
- Doctor burnout has become an epidemic in the world of medicine. Recent changes in record keeping, insurance, and technological advances, as well

as increased expenses, have made it more stressful and frustrating than ever before.

- All this "business end" is not what they signed up for—they are there to look after sick people. This makes many doctors tired, bitter, and demoralized, and they may be considering moving to a more rewarding career.
- Burnout is an erosion of the soul. It is not listed among the psychiatric diagnoses—and there is no stigma attached to it.
- The more sensitive and conscientious the doctor is, the more prone she or he is to burnout because they care deeply about their mission. Bad news: their unselfishness and kindness can backfire, and they end up getting sick themselves.
- Many doctors don't even know they are sick and may not be receiving any treatment for their depression.
- Physicians are very private about any treatment.
- Spouses should be included in their loved one's treatment and kept abreast of what they are doing.
- Psychiatric illnesses are always hard to accept— and often even harder for a doctor than others.
- Stigma: Because a doctor's life has been so defined by achievement—he or she has difficulty being perceived as a failure or a burden. We need to show doctors more compassion.

- Often the doctor's life changes as he or she struggles with deep depression triggered by loss or stress, panicky thinking about ruin, loss of their medical license, etc.

Betsy's Final Thought:

We must continue to be candid and rigorous—and we must keep talking about a subject that, sadly, is not going away. When that day comes, and hopefully it will, we can be quiet. Until then, we must be brave when exploring darkness—because it is there we will discover the boundless power of our light.

Helping patients is why these people became doctors. I now feel it is time to help them.

Acknowledgment

So many people have helped me along this awful journey and helped me with this book. My life can only be described as serendipitous—or as I like to think, *guided by God*. Everyone placed in my life was carefully done so by Him for me.

First of all, to Grady, Gavin, and Sophie, I so wish this life-altering event had never happened to our family. My heart breaks for you, and it breaks for your dad. There was no man on earth who ever loved his kids more than your dad loved you. You have taught me so much over the past twenty years. I say it all the time but it's true: God blessed me the most by making me your mom. I love you.

To my parents, thank you for teaching me about God when I was a small child. Without my belief in Him, I'm not sure where I'd be. Thank you for the continued support of me and the children. You have been the best parents a girl could ever ask for. My family is the best there is, a special thank you to Bo, Silla, Chris, and Diane, there are no adequate words in the English language to thank you for all you've done for us. And I'd be remiss if I failed to thank Bruce and Elaine for raising such an amazing son, father, husband, and best friend. He will forever be missed.

To my Minnesota childhood girlfriends and my North Carolina girlfriends, and my college bestie, what can I say? You all carried me through one of the most difficult times of my life. As I learned, some friends choose to abandon you. You all (or y'all as they say in the South) chose to jump in and help me keep my head above water on days when I thought I'd drown. I love each of you more than you could ever know.

Thank you to my book club. The past twenty years of reading with you has only enhanced my love of books, memoirs, stories, and learning. It has been a joy to do life with you. You're all so important to me, and I appreciate your input on this book about a man you all knew in one capacity or another.

To my instructors at the gym, Grace Women, to my therapist, my suicide support group, to KB and The Fixer you're all proof of remarkable relationships formed out of kindness. You never know what another person is going through. Thank you for being kind to me.

Thank you to my book advisor and editor, Connie Anderson. Connie took on the difficult task of taking my journals and turning them into an actual book. I'll forever be grateful. She took out *all* (well almost all) of my swear words. Believe me, that alone was a big undertaking. Thank you, Connie, without you this memoir would not have come to fruition. I have no doubt it will help our health care professionals. *The story itself is a call to action.*

Thank you to my publisher Ann Aubitz and to the people at Kirk House Publishers. Let's be honest here, I had no idea how to write a book or the process associated with it. Thank you for not only your guidance but patience. I tell everyone that I'm a real estate agent not a writer but by the Grace of God, I am now an author. I appreciate your help.

Betsy Gall Contact Information
For more details, please follow her:
Facebook.com/Betsy Gall
Instagram Betsygall1
Email: Betsygall1@gmail.com

Resources

National Suicide Prevention Lifeline
1-800-273-8255
Text "HOME" to 741741
SuicidePreventionLifeline.org